George Laurence Gomme

**Ethnology on Folklore**

George Laurence Gomme

**Ethnology on Folklore**

ISBN/EAN: 9783744782630

Printed in Europe, USA, Canada, Australia, Japan

Cover: Foto ©Thomas Meinert / pixelio.de

More available books at **www.hansebooks.com**

# ETHNOLOGY IN FOLKLORE

BY

GEORGE LAURENCE GOMME, F. S. A.

PRESIDENT OF THE FOLKLORE SOCIETY, ETC.

NEW YORK
D. APPLETON AND COMPANY
1892

# PREFACE.

I HAVE sought in this book to ascertain and set forth the principles upon which folklore may be classified, in order to arrive at some of the results which should follow from its study. That it contains ethnological elements might be expected by all who have paid any attention to recent research, but no attempt has hitherto been made to set these elements down categorically and to examine the conclusions which are to be drawn from them.

It is due to the large and increasing band of folklore devotees that the uses of folklore should be brought forward. The scoffer at these studies is apt to have it all his own way so long as the bulk of the books published on folklore contain nothing but collected examples of tales, customs, and superstitions, arranged for no purpose but that of putting the facts pleasantly before readers. But, more than this, recent research tends to show the increasing importance of bringing into proper order, within reasonable time, all the evidence that is available from different sources upon any given subject of inquiry. Looked at in this light, ethnology has great claims upon the student. The science of culture has almost refused to deal with it, and has been content with noting only a few landmarks which occur here and there along the lines of development traceable in the elements of human culture. But the science of history has of late been busy with many problems of ethnological importance, and has for this purpose turned sometimes to craniology, sometimes to archæology, sometimes to philology, but rarely to folklore. If folklore, then, does contain ethnological facts, it is time that they should be disclosed, and that the method of discovering them should be placed before scholars.

Of course, my attempt in this direction must not be looked upon in any sense as an exhaustive treatment of the subject, and I am not vain enough to expect that all my conclusions will be accepted. I believe that the time has come when every item of folklore should be docketed and put into its proper place, and I hope I have done something toward this end in the following pages. When complete classification is attempted some of the items of folklore will be found useless enough. But most of them will help us to understand more of the development of thought than any other subject; and many of them will, if my reading of the evidence is correct, take us back, not only to stages in the history of human thought, but to the people who have yielded up the struggle of their minds to the modern student of man and his strivings.

At the risk of crowding the pages with footnotes, I have been careful to give references to all my authorities for items of folklore, because so much depends upon the value of the authority used in these studies. I believe they are all quoted accurately, but shall always be glad to know of any corrections or additions.

Professor Rhys has kindly read through my proofs, and I am very grateful for the considerable service he has thereby rendered me.

BARNES COMMON, S. W., *March*, 1892.

# CONTENTS.

# ETHNOLOGY IN FOLKLORE.

## CHAPTER I.

### SURVIVAL AND DEVELOPMENT.

THERE has grown up of late years a subject of inquiry—first antiquarian merely, and now scientific—into the peasant and local elements in modern culture, and this subject has not inaptly been termed "folklore." Almost always at the commencement of a new study much is done by eager votaries which has to be undone as soon as settled work is undertaken, and it happens, I think, that because the elements of folklore are so humble and unpretentious, because they have to be sought for in the peasant's cottage or fields, in the children's nursery, or from the lips of old gaffers and gammers, that unusual difficulties have beset the student of folklore. Not only has he to undo any futile work that stands in the way of his special inquiry, but he has to attempt the rebuilding of his edifice in face of contrasts frequently drawn between the elements which make up his subject and those supposed more dignified elements with which the historian, the archæologist, and the philologist have to deal.

The essential characteristic of folklore is that it consists of beliefs, customs, and traditions which are far behind civilization in their intrinsic value to man, though they exist under the cover of a civilized nationality. This estimate of the position of folklore with reference to civilization suggests that its constituent elements are survivals of a condition of human thought more backward, and therefore more ancient, than that in which they are discovered.

Except to the students of anthropology, the fact of the existence of survivals of older culture in our midst is not readily grasped or understood. Historians have been so engrossed with the political and commercial progress of nations that it is not easy to determine what room they would make in the world for the non-progressive portion of the population. And yet the history of every country must begin with the races who have occupied it. Almost everywhere in Europe there are traces, in some form or other, of a powerful race of people, unknown in modern history, who have left material remains of their culture to later ages. The Celts have written their history on the map of Europe in a scarcely less marked manner than the Teutons, and we still talk of Celtic countries and Teutonic countries. On the other hand, Greek and Roman civilizations have in some countries and some districts an almost unbroken record, in spite of much modification and development. With such an amalgam in the background, historians have scarcely ever failed to draw the picture of European civilization in deep colors, tinted according to their bias in favor of a Celtic, or Teutonic, or classical origin. But the picture of uncivilization within the same area has not been drawn. The story always is of the advanced part of nations,* though even here it occurs to me that very frequently the terminology is still more in advance of the facts, so that while every one has heard a great deal of the conditions of civilization, very few people have any adequate idea of the unadvanced lines of European life.

It will be seen that I accentuate the contrast between civilization and uncivilization within the same area, and the purpose of this accentuation will be seen when the significant difference in origin is pointed out.

Dr. Tylor states that the elevation of some branches of a race over the rest more often happens as the result of foreign than of native action. "Civilization is a plant much oftener propagated than developed," he says.† How true this remark is will be recognized by any one familiar with the main outlines of the history of civilization, ancient or modern. An axiom formulated by Sir Arthur Mitchell that "no man in isolation can become civilized," may be extended to societies. Whether in the case of Roman, Greek, Assyrian, Egyptian, or even Chinese civilization, a point has always

---

* Some confirmation of this from classical history was pointed out by Dr. Beddoe in his address to the Anthrop. Inst. (see *Journal*, xx, 355).

† *Primitive Culture*, i, 48.

been reached at which scholars have had to turn their attention from the land where these civilizations were consummated to some other land or people, whose influence in building them up is detected in considerable force. And so it is in the Western world. There are few scholars now who advocate the theory of an advanced Celtic or Teutonic civilization. Roman law, Greek philosophy and art, and Christian religion and ethics have combined in producing a civilization which is essentially foreign to the soil whereon it now flourishes.

But with uncivilization the case is very different. Arrested by forces which we can not but identify with the civilizations which have at various times swept over it, it seems imbedded in the soil where it was first transplanted, and has no power or chance of fresh propagation. There is absolutely no evidence, in spite of allegations to the contrary, of the introduction of uncivilized culture into countries already in possession of a higher culture. And yet it is found everywhere and is kept alive by the sanction of tradition—the traditional observance of what has always been observed, simply because it has always been observed. Thus, after the law of the land has been complied with and the marriage knot has been effectually tied, traditional custom imposes certain rites which may without exaggeration be styled irrational, rude, and barbarous. After the Church has conducted to its last resting-place the corpse of the departed, traditional belief necessitates the performance of some magic rite which may with propriety be considered not only rude, but savage. Underneath the law and the Church, therefore, the emblems of the foreign civilization, lie the traditional custom and belief, the attributes of the native uncivilization. And the native answer to any inquiry as to why these irrational elements exist is invariably the same—"They are obliged to do it for antiquity or custom's sake";* they do it because they believe in it, "as things that had been and were real, and not as creations of the fancy or old-wives' tales and babble." Even after real belief has passed away the habit continues; there is "a sort of use and wont in it which, though in a certain sense honored in its observance, it is felt, in some sort of indirect, unmeditated, unvolitional sort of way, would not be dishonored in the breach." †

The significant answer of the peasant, when questioned as to the cause of his observing rude and irrational customs, of entertaining strange and uncouth beliefs, marks a very important characteristic of what has been so conveniently termed folklore. All that the peasantry practice, believe, and relate on the strength of immemorial custom sanctioned by unbroken succes-

* Buchan's *St. Kilda*, p. 35. Mr. Atkinson gives much the same testimony of Yorkshire. Inquiring as to a usage practiced on a farm, the answer was: "Ay, there's many as dis it yet. My au'd father did it. But it's sae many years syne it must be about wore out by now, and I shall have to dee it again."—*Forty Years in a Moorland Parish*, p. 62. Miss Gordon Cumming's example of the force of custom in her book on the *Hebrides* is very amusing (p. 209).

† Atkinson, *op. cit.*, pp. 63, 72.

sion from one generation to another, has a value of peculiar significance so soon as it is perceived that the genealogy of each custom, belief, or legend in nearly all cases goes back for its commencing point to some fact in the history of the people which has escaped the notice of the historian. No act of legislation, no known factor in the records of history, can be pointed to as the origin of the practices, beliefs, and traditions of the peasantry, which exist in such great abundance. They are dateless and parentless when reckoned by the facts of civilization. They are treasured and reverenced, kept secret from Church, law, and legislation, handed down by tradition, when reckoned by the facts of peasant life. That these dateless elements in the national culture are also very frequently rude, irrational, and senseless only adds to the significance of their existence and to the necessity of some adequate explanation of that existence being supplied.

No one would pretend that modern civilization consciously admits within its bounds practices and beliefs like those enshrined in folklore, and few will argue that modern civilization is an evolution in direct line from such rude originals. The theory that best meets the case is that they are to be identified with the rude culture of ancient Europe, which has been swept over by waves of higher culture from foreign sources, that nearly everywhere the rude culture has succumbed to the force of these waves, but has nevertheless here and there stood firm.

Now, these being the conditions under which the survivals of ancient customs and beliefs exist, we have to note that they can not by any possibility develop. Having been arrested in their progress by some outside force, their development ceases. They continue, generation after generation, either in a state of absolute crystallization, or they decay and split up into fragments; they become degraded into mere symbolism or whittled down into mere superstition; they drop back from a position of general use or observance by a whole community into the personal observance of some few individuals, or of a class; they cease to affect the general conduct of the people, and become isolated and secret. Thus in folklore there is no development from one stage of culture to a higher one.

These considerations serve to show how distinctly folklore is marked off from the political and social surroundings in which it is imbedded, and all questions as to its origin must therefore be a specific inquiry dealing with all the facts. The answer of the peasant already given shows the road which must be taken for such a purpose. We must travel back from generation to generation of peasant life until a stage is reached where isolated beliefs and customs of the peasantry of to-day are found to occupy a foremost place in tribal or national custom. To do this, the aid of comparative custom and belief must be invoked. As Mr. Lang has so well expressed it: "When an apparently irrational and anomalous custom is found in any country, the method is to look for a country where a similar practice is no longer irrational or anomalous, but in harmony with the manners and ideas of the people among whom it prevails." * Here, then, will be found the true meaning of customs and beliefs which exist uselessly in the midst of civilization. Their relationship to other customs and beliefs at a similar level of culture will also be ascertained. When we subtract any particular custom of an uncivilized people from the general body of its associated customs, in order to compare it with a similar custom existing in isolated form in civilization, we are careful to note what other customs exist side by side with it in corelationship. These are its natural adhesions, so to speak, and by following them out we may also discover natural adhesions in folklore. But this is not all. The work of comparison having been accomplished with reference to the group of customs and beliefs in natural adhesion to each other, there will be found in folklore a large residuum of manifest inconsistencies. I am inclined to lay considerable stress upon these inconsistencies in folklore. They have been noted frequently enough, but have not been adequately explained. They have been set down to the curious twistings of the human mind when indulging in mythic thought. But I shall have another explanation to give, which will rest upon the facts of ethnology.

Is it true, then, that the process of comparison be-

---

* *Custom and Myth*, p. 21.

tween the elements of folklore and the customs and beliefs of uncivilized or savage people can be carried out to any considerable extent, or is it limited to a few isolated and exceptional examples? It is obvious that this question is a vital one. It will be partly answered in the following pages; but in the mean time it may be pointed out that although anthropologists have very seldom penetrated far into the realms of folklore, they have frequently noted that the beliefs and customs of savages find a close parallel among peasant beliefs and practices in Europe. More than once in the pages of Dr. Tylor, Sir John Lubbock, Mr. McLennan, and others, it is to be observed that the author turns aside from the consideration of the savage phenomena he is dealing with to draw attention to the close resemblance which they bear to some fragments of folklore—"the series ends as usual in the folklore of the civilized world" are Dr. Tylor's expressive words.*

I do not want to lay too much stress upon words which may, perhaps, be considered by some to have been only a happy literary expression for interpreting an isolated group of facts immediately under the notice of the author. But that they are not to be so considered, and that they convey a real condition of things in the science of culture, may be tested by an examination of Dr. Tylor's work, and I set them forth in order to fix upon them as one of the most important axioms in folk-

---

* *Primitive Culture*, i, 407.

lore research. This axiom must, indeed, be constantly borne in mind as we wend our way through the various items of folklore in the following pages, and it will help to illustrate how much need there is to establish once and for all what place the several groups of folklore occupy in the culture series.

This way of expressing the relationship between savage culture and folklore suggests many important considerations when applied to a particular area. If peasant culture and savage culture are now at many points in close contact, how far may we go back to find the beginning of that contact? Must we not dig down beneath each stratum of overlying higher culture and remove all the superincumbent mass before we can arrive at the original layer? There seems to be no other course open. The forces that keep certain beliefs and ideas of man in civilized countries within the recognizable limits of savage culture, and continue them in this state generation after generation, can not be derived from the nature of individual men or women, or the results would be less systematic and evenly distributed, and would be liable to disappear and reappear according to circumstances. They must, therefore, act collectively, and must form an essential part of the beliefs and ideas which they govern.

I do not know whether my use of the terms of geology in the attempt to state the position of folklore in relationship to the higher cultures is unduly suggestive, but it undoubtedly puts before the inquirer into the origins of folklore the suggestion that the unnamed forces which are so obviously present must to a very great extent be identical with race. It can not be that the fragments of rude and irrational practices in civilized countries arise from the poor and peasant class having been in the habit of constantly borrowing the practices and ideas of savages, because, among other reasons against such a theory, this borrowed culture must to a corresponding degree have displaced the practices and ideas of civilization. All the evidence goes to prove that the peasantry have inherited rude and irrational practices and ideas from savage predecessors—practices and ideas which have never been displaced by civilization. To deal adequately with these survivals is the accepted province of the science of folklore, and it must therefore account for their existence, must point out the causes for their arrested development and the causes for their long continuance in a state of crystallization or degradation after the stoppage has been effected. And I put it that these requirements can only be met by an hypothesis which directly appeals to the racial elements in the population. There is first the arresting force, identified with the higher culture sweeping over the lower; there is then the continuing force, identified with the lower culture.

Let us see how this works out. The most important fact to note in the examination of each fragment of folklore is the point of arrested development. Has the custom or belief, surviving by the side of much higher culture, been arrested in its development while it was simply a savage custom or belief; when it was a barbaric custom or belief at a higher level than savagery; when it was a national custom or belief discarded by the governing class and obtaining locally?

Translating these factors in the characteristics of each item of folklore into terms of ethnology, it appears that we have at all events sufficient data for considering custom or belief which survives in the savage form as of different ethnic origin from custom or belief which survives in higher forms.

But if the incoming civilizations flowing over lower levels of culture in any given area have been many, there will be as many stages of arrestment in the folklore of that area, and in so far as each incoming civilization represents an ethnic distinction, the different stages of survival in folklore would also represent an ethnic distinction.

The incoming civilizations in modern Europe are not all ethnic, as the most impressive has been Christianity. It is impossible for the most casual reader to have left unnoticed the frequent evidence which is afforded of folklore being older than Christianity—having, in fact, been arrested in its development by Christianity. But at the back of Christianity the incoming civilizations have been true ethnic distinctions, Scandinavian, Teutonic, Roman, Celtic, overflowing each other, and all of them superimposed upon the original uncivilization of the prehistoric races of non-Aryan stock.

It appears to me that the clash of these races is still represented in folklore. It is not possible at the commencement of studies like the present to unravel all the various elements, and particularly is it impossible with our present knowledge to discriminate to any great extent between the several branches of the Aryan race.* The biography of each item of Aryan custom and belief has not been examined into like the biography of each word of the Aryan tongue. This will have to be done before the work of the comparative sciences has been completed. But even with our limited knowledge of Aryan culture, it does seem possible to mark in folklore traces of an arrested development at the point of savagery, side by side with a further development which has not been arrested until well within the area of Aryan culture.

This dual element in folklore, represented by a series of well-marked inconsistencies in peasant custom and belief, proves that the stages of development at which the several items of folklore have been arrested are not at the same level; and they could not therefore have been produced by *one* arresting power. Thus the conflict between paganism and Christianity is so obviously

* Miss Burne has, I think, successfully distinguished between Welsh and English origins in the folklore of Shropshire (see her *Shropshire Folklore*, p. 462, and the map). And Lord Teignmouth suggested that the prejudice against swine held by the Western Highlanders and Hebrideans indicates a difference of race from the Orcadians, who have no such prejudice.—*Islands of Scotland*, i, 276.

a source to which the phenomenon of pagan survivals might be traced, that almost exclusive attention has been paid to it. It would account for one line of arrestment. It would have stopped the further progress of Aryan beliefs and customs represented in the Teutonic, Celtic, and Scandinavian culture, and it would correspondingly account for survivals at this point of arrestment. Survivals at a point of arrestment further back in the development of culture than the Aryan stage must have already existed under the pressure of Aryan culture. They must have been produced by a stoppage antecedent to Christianity, and must be identified, therefore, with the arrival of the Aryan race into a country occupied by non-Ayrans.

If, then, I can show that there are, primarily, two lines of arrested development to be traced in folklore, these two lines must be represented the one by savage culture, which is not Aryan, the other by Aryan culture.

It must, however, be pointed out that the relationship between what may be termed savagery and Aryan culture has not been formally set forth, though it seems certain that there is a considerable gap between the two, caused by a definite advance in culture by the Aryan race before its dispersal from the primitive home. This advance is the result of development, and where development takes place the originals from which it has proceeded disappear in the new forms thus produced. To adopt the terms of the manufactory, the original forms would have been all used up in the process of production. Hence, none of the savage culture from which may be traced the beginnings of Aryan culture can have survived among Aryan people. If items of it are found to exist side by side with Aryan culture in any country, such a phenomenon must be due to causes which have brought Aryan and savage races into close dwelling with each other, and can in no sense be interpreted as original forms existing side by side with those which have developed from them. I put this important proposition forward without hesitation as a sound conclusion to be derived from the study of human culture. It is not possible in these pages to give the tests which I have applied to prove it, because they belong to the statistical side of our study, but I adduce Dr. Tylor's notable attempt to work out the method of studying institutions as sufficient evidence for my immediate purpose.*

These somewhat dry technicalities are necessary in order to explain the basis of our present inquiry. Some years ago Sir John Lubbock said: "It can not be doubted that the careful study of manners and customs, traditions and superstitions, will eventually solve many difficult problems of ethnology. This mode of research, however, requires to be used with great caution, and has, in fact, led to many erroneous conclusions. . . . Much careful study will therefore be required before this class of evidence can be used with safety, though I doubt not

* See *Journ. Anthrop. Inst.*

that eventually it will be found most instructive." * It is singular what little progress has been made in this branch of work since this paragraph was written, and, indeed, how very generally the subject has been neglected, although now and again a passage in some of our best authorities suggests the necessity for some research being undertaken into the question of race distinctions in custom and myth. Mr. Lang, for instance, when asking how the pure religion of Artemis had developed from the cult of a ravening she-bear, puts the case forcibly thus: "Here is a moment in mythical and religious evolution which almost escapes inquiry. . . . How did the complex theory of the nature of Artemis arise? What was its growth? At what precise hour did it emancipate itself on the whole from the lower savage creeds? Or how was it developed out of their unpromising materials? The science of mythology may perhaps never find a key to these obscure problems." † But I think the science of folklore may go far toward the desired end. Its course would be to take note of the points of arrested development, and to classify what has survived in the savage stage and what

* *Origin of Civilization*, p. 4. Dalyell, in some of his acute observations on superstition, says that he thought "it might be possible to connect the modern inhabitants of Scotland with the ancient tribes of other countries, and to trace their descent through the medium of superstitions."—*Darker Superstitions of Scotland*, p. 236. In 1835, when this book was published, this way of putting the relationship of one people with another had not been abolished by the work accomplished by anthropology.

† *Myth, Ritual, and Religion*, ii, 215.

is represented in the higher stages as being of two distinct ethnic origins, and its conclusion would be that Artemis "succeeded to and threw her protection over an ancient worship of the animal," and that therefore the cult of Artemis and the local cults connected with it are as to race of different origin, and may both be called Greek in reference only to their final state of amalgamation in the land which the Aryan Greeks conquered and named.

One of the principal features of the Artemis cult is the extremely savage form of some of the local rituals, and it will frequently be found that localities preserve relics of a people much older than those who now inhabit them. Thus the daubing of the bridegroom's feet with soot in Scotland,* the painting with black substance of one of the characters in the Godiva ride at Southam in Warwickshire,† the daubing of the naked body in the Dionysiac mysteries of the Greeks, are explained by none of the requirements of civilization, but by practices to be found in Africa and elsewhere. The ancestry of the Scottish, Warwickshire, and Greek customs, therefore, may be traced back to a people on the level of culture with African savages.

But when we come to ask who were the people who introduced this savage custom, we are for the first time conscious of the important question of race. Are we

---

* Gregor, *Folklore of Northeast Scotland*, p. 90; Rogers, *Social Life in Scotland*, i, 110.

† Hartland, *Science of Fairy Tales*, p. 85.

compelled to call them Scotchmen, Englishmen, or Greek? Mr. Lang and Mr. Frazer would, I believe, answer "Yes"; * and they are followed, consciously or unconsciously, by all other folklorists. I shall attempt a somewhat different answer, the construction and proof of which will occupy the following pages. But as a preliminary justification for such a course I quote Dr. Tylor's warning: "The evidence of locality may be misleading as to race. A traveler in Greenland coming on the ruined stone buildings at Kakortok would not argue justly that the Esquimaux are degenerate descendants of ancestors capable of such architecture, for, in fact, these are the remains of a church and baptistry built by the ancient Scandinavian settlers." † Exactly. The long-chambered barrows, hill earthworks and cultivation sites, cave dwellings and palæolithic implements, are not attributable to Celt or Teuton. Can we, then, without substantial reason and without special inquiry, say that a custom or belief, however rude and savage, is Celtic, or Teutonic, or Greek, simply because it is extant in a country occupied in historic times by people speaking the language of any of these peoples?

A negative answer must clearly be returned to this question. The subject, no doubt, is a difficult one when thought of in connection with European countries. But in India, less leveled by civilization than the Western world, the ethnographer, with very little effort, can de-

* Consult Mr. Lang's *Custom and Myth*, p. 26.

† *Primitive Culture*, i. 51.

tect ethnic distinctions in custom and belief. Stone worship in India, for instance, is classed by Dr. Tylor as "a survival of a rite belonging originally to a low civilization, probably a rite of the rude indigenes of the land."* But are not survivals of stone worship in Europe similarly to be classed as belonging to the rude indigenes of the land? The log that stood for Artemis in Eubœa, the stake that represented Pallas Athene, the unwrought stone at Hyettos which represented Herakles, the thirty stones which the Pharæans worshiped for the gods, and the stone representing the Thespian Eros, may, with equal propriety, be classed as survivals of the non-Aryan indigenes of Greece. What may be rejected as belonging to the Aryans of India because there is distinct evidence of its belonging to the non-Aryans, can not be accepted without even an inquiry as belonging to the Aryans of Greece. No doubt the difficulty of tracing direct evidence of the early non-Aryan races of Europe is very great, but it is no way out of the difficulty to ignore the fact that there exist survivals of savage culture which would readily be classified as non-Aryan if it so happened that there now existed certain tribes of non-Aryan people to whom they might be allotted. On the contrary, the existence of survivals of savage culture is *prima facie* evidence of the existence of races to whom this culture belonged and from whom it has descended. I do not mean to suggest

---

* *Primitive Culture*, ii, 150.

that in all places where items of non-Aryan culture have survived people of non-Aryan race have survived. Old races disappear while old customs last—carried on by successors, but not necessarily by descendants. The genealogy of folklore carries us back to the race of people from whom it derives its parentage, but it does not necessarily carry back the genealogy of modern peasantry to the same race. This latter part of the question is a matter for ethnologists to deal with, and it may be that some unlooked-for results are yet to be derived from a close study of ethnic types in our local populations in relation to the folklore preserved by them.

# CHAPTER II.

## ETHNIC ELEMENTS IN CUSTOM AND RITUAL.

It is necessary now to test by the evidence of actual example the hypothesis that race distinction is the true explanation of the strange inconsistency which is met with in folklore. There should be evidence somewhere, if such a hypothesis is tenable, that the almost unchecked conclusions of scholars are not correct when they argue that because a custom or belief, however savage and rude, obtained in Rome or in Greece, in German or Celtic countries of modern Europe, it is Roman, Greek, German, or Celtic throughout all its variations.

For this purpose an example must be found which will comply with certain conditions. It must obtain in a country overlorded by an Aryan people, and still occupied by non-Aryan indigenes. It must consist of distinct divisions, showing the part taken by Aryans and the part taken by non-Aryans. And as such an example can scarcely be found in Europe, it must at least be paralleled in the folklore of Europe, if not in all its constituent parts, at all events in all the essential details.

Such an example is to be found in India. I shall

first of all set forth the principal points which are necessary to note in this example in the words, as nearly as possible, of the authority I quote, so that the comments which it will be necessary to make upon it may not interfere with the evidence as it stands originally recorded.

The festival of the village goddess is honored throughout all southern India and in other parts, from Berar to the extreme east of Bustar and in Mysore. She is generally adored in the form of an unshapely stone covered with vermilion. A small altar is erected behind the temple of the village goddess to a rural god named Pótraj. All the members of the village community take part in the festival, with the hereditary district officers, many of them Brahmans.

An examination of the ritual belonging to this village festival enables us not only to detect the presence of race distinctions and of practices which belong to them, but compels us tó conclude that the whole ceremony originated in race distinctions.

The festival is under the guidance and management of the Parias, who act as officiating priests. With them are included the Mangs or workers in leather, the Asádis or Dásaris, Paria dancing-girls devoted to the service of the temple, the musician in attendance on them, who acts as a sort of jester or buffoon, and a functionary called Pótraj, who officiates as *pujári* to the god of the same name. The shepherds or Dhangars of the neighboring villages are also invited. Of these the Parias are an outcast people, degraded in the extreme, and always excluded from the village and from contact with the inhabitants. They are identified with the Paraya, a southern aboriginal tribe nearly allied to the Gonds. The shepherd caste is found throughout the greater part of the Dekkan in detached communities, called Kurumbars, Kurubars, and Dhangars, in different parts of India. These are the non-Aryan races who take part in this Aryan village festival; they occupy the foremost place during the festival, and at its termination they retire to their hamlets outside the town and resume their humble servile character. From these facts Sir W. Elliot has deduced as probable conclusions that the earliest known inhabitants of southern India were an aboriginal race, who worshiped local divinities, the tutelary gods of earth, hill, grove, and boundaries, etc., and that this worship has been blended in practice with that of the Aryan overlords.

The principal parts of the ritual which it is useful for us to note are as follows: The Pótraj priest was armed with a long whip, to which at various parts of the ceremony divine honors were paid. The sacred buffalo was turned loose when a calf, and allowed to feed and roam about the village. On the second day this animal was thrown down before the goddess, its head struck off by a single blow, and placed in front of the shrine with one foreleg thrust into its mouth. Around were placed vessels containing the different cereals, and hard by a heap of mixed grains with a drill-plow in the center. The carcass was then cut up into small pieces, and each cultivator received a portion to bury in his field. The blood and offal were collected into a large basket over which some pots of cooked food had previously been broken, and Pótraj, taking a live kid, hewed it to pieces over the whole. The mess was then mixed together, and the basket being placed on the head of a naked Mang, he ran off with it, flinging the contents into the air and scattering them right and left as an offering to the evil spirits, and followed by the other Parias. The whole party made the circuit of the village.

The third and fourth days were devoted to private offerings. On the former, all the inhabitants of caste who had vowed animals to the goddess during the preceding three years for the welfare of their families or the fertility of their fields brought the buffaloes or sheep to the Paria *pujári*, who struck off their heads. The fourth day is appropriated exclusively to the offerings of the Parias. In this way some fifty or sixty buffaloes and several hundred sheep were slain, and the heads piled up in two great heaps. Many women on these days walked naked to the temple in fulfillment of vows, but they were covered with leaves and boughs of trees, and surrounded by their female relations and friends.

On the fifth and last day the whole community marched in procession with music to the temple, and offered a concluding sacrifice at the Pótraj altar. A lamb was concealed close by. The Pótraj having found it after a pretended search, struck it simply with his whip, which he then placed upon it, and making several passes with his hands rendered it insensible. His hands were then tied behind his back by the *pujári*, and the whole party began to dance round him with noisy shouts. Pótraj joined in the excitement, and he soon came fully under the influence of the deity. He was led up, still bound, to the place where the lamb lay motionless. He rushed at it, seized it with his teeth, tore through the skin, and ate into its throat. When it was quite dead he was lifted up, a dishful of the meat-offering was presented to him; he thrust his bloody face into it, and it was then with the remains of the lamb buried beside the altar. Meantime his hands were untied, and he fled the place.

The rest of the party now adjourned to the front of the temple, where the heap of grain deposited the first day was divided among all the cultivators, to be buried by each one in his field with the bit of flesh. After this a distribution of the piled-up heads was made by the hands of the musician or Raniga. About forty sheep's heads were given to certain privileged persons, among which two were allotted to the sircar. For the rest a general scramble took place—paiks, shepherds, Parias, and many boys and men of good caste were soon rolling in the mass of putrid gore. The scramble for the buffalo-heads was confined to the Parias. Whoever was fortunate enough to secure one of either kind carried it off and buried it in his field.

The proceedings terminated by a procession round the boundaries of the village lands, preceded by the goddess and the head of the sacred buffalo carried on the head of one of the Mangs. All order and propriety now ceased. Raniga began to abuse the goddess in the foulest language; he then turned his fury against the Government, the head man of the village, and every one who fell in his way. The Parias and Asádis attacked the most respectable and gravest citizens, and laid hold of Brahmans, Lingayats, and zamindars without scruple. The dancing-women jumped on their shoulders, the shepherds beat the big drum, and universal license prevailed.

On reaching a little temple sacred to the goddess of boundaries, they halted to make some offerings and to bury the sacred head. As soon as it was covered the uproar began again. Raniga became more foul-mouthed than ever, and the head men, the Government officers, and others tried to pacify him by giving him small copper coins. This went on till, the circuit being completed, all dispersed.*

It has been worth while transcribing here this elaborate description of a veritable folk drama because it is necessary to have before us the actual details of the ritual observed and the beliefs expressed before we can properly attempt a comparison.

We must now ascertain how far European folklore

* Sir W. Elliot, in *Journ. Ethnological Soc.*, N. S. i, 97–100.

tallies with the ceremonies observed in this Indian village festival. If there is a strong line of parallel between the Indian ceremonies and some ceremonies still observed in Europe as survivals of a forgotten and unrecognized cult, I shall argue that ceremonies which are demonstrably non-Aryan in India, even in the presence of Aryan people, must in origin have been non-Aryan in Europe, though the race from whom they have descended is not at present identified by ethnologists.

I shall not at this juncture dwell upon the unshapen stone which represented the goddess. Its parallels exist throughout the whole range of early religions, and, as we have already seen, appear in the folklore of Europe. As the Kafirs of India say of the stones they use, "This stands for God, but we know not his shape."* All the more need for it to be unshapen by men's hands, and the history of the sacred use of monoliths commences at this point † and ends with the sculptured glories of Greece.‡ Later on some special forms of stone deities will be noticed; it is the use of a stone as a sort of altar of the goddess, who is not identical with it, and the recognition of stone worship as a part of the aboriginal cult, and not Aryan,# which interests us now.

This stone is the place of sacrifice to the harvest

---

* Latham, *Descriptive Ethnology*, ii, 240.

† *Cf.* Robertson Smith, *Religion of the Semites*, pp. 186–195; Ellis, *Ewe-speaking People*, p. 28.

‡ See an able article in the *Archæological Review*, ii, 167–184, by Mr. Farnell.

\# *Arch. Survey of India*, xvi, 141.

goddess, and the ceremonial observed at the Indian festival directs us at once to the local observances connected with the cult of Dionysus. The Cretans in representing the sufferings and death of Dionysus tore a bull to pieces with their teeth; indeed, says Mr. Frazer, quoting the authority of Euripides, the rending and devouring of live bulls and calves appears to have been a regular feature of the Dionysiac rites, and his worshipers also rent in pieces a live goat and devoured it raw. At Tenedos the new-born calf sacrificed to the god was shod in buskins, and the mother cow was tended like a woman in childbed—sure proof of the symbolization of human sacrifice, which indeed actually took place at Chios and at Orchomenus.* These are virtually the same practices as those now going on in India, and the identification is confirmed by the facts (1) that Dionysus is sometimes represented to his worshipers by his head only—a counterpart of the sacred character of the head in the Indian rites; (2) that the sacrificer of the calf at Tenedos was, after the accomplishment of the rite, driven out from the place and stoned—a counterpart of the Pótraj fleeing the place after the sacrifice of the lamb in the Indian ceremony; and (3) that the female worshipers of Dionysus attended in a nude state, crowned with garlands, and their bodies daubed over with clay and dirt—a counterpart of the female votaries who attended

* Mr. Frazer has collected all the references to these facts in his *Golden Bough*, i, 326–329; see also Lang, *Custom and Myth*, ii, 231–234.

naked and surrounded with branches of trees at the Indian festival.

I have selected this cult of the Greeks for the purpose of comparing it with the non-Aryan ceremonial of India, because it has recently been examined with all the wealth of illustration and comparison by two such great authorities as Mr. Lang and Mr. Frazer. They have stripped it of most of the fanciful surroundings with which German and English mythologists have recently loaded it, and once more restored the local rituals and the central myth as the true sources from which to obtain information as to its origin. At almost every point the details of the local rituals are comparable, not to Greek conceptions of Dionysus, "a youth with clusters of golden hair and in his dark eyes the grace of Aphrodite," but to the ferocious and barbaric practices of savages. Then where is the evidence of the Greek origin of these local observances? Greek religious thought was far in advance of them. It stooped to admit them within the rites of the god Dionysus, but in this act there was a conscious borrowing by Greeks of something lower in the stage of culture than Greek culture, and that something has been characterized by a recent commentator as appertaining to "the divinities of the common people." * This is very near

* Dyer's *Gods of Greece*, p. 123. Mr. Dyer says: "The most painstaking security, the minutest examination of such evidence as may be had, will never disentangle completely, never make perfectly plain, just what elements constituted the Dionysus first

to the race distinction I am in search of. The common people of Crete, Tenedos, Chios, and Orchomenus were not necessarily Aryan Greeks, and, judged by their savage customs, they most likely stood in the same relationship to the Aryans of Greece as the Parias of the Indian villages stand to their Aryan overlords.

I pass from Greek folklore to English. It would be easy to extend research right across Europe, especially with Mr. Frazer's aid, but it is scarcely necessary. A Whitsuntide custom in the parish of King's Teignton, Devonshire, is thus described: A lamb is drawn about the parish on Whitsun Monday in a cart covered with garlands of lilac, laburnum, and other flowers, when persons are requested to give something toward the animal and attendant expenses; on Tuesday it is then killed and roasted whole in the middle of the village. The lamb is then sold in slices to the poor at a cheap rate. The origin of the custom is forgotten, but a tradition, supposed to trace back to heathen days, is to this effect: The village suffered from a dearth of water,

---

worshiped in early Greece. His character was composite from the moment Greeks worshiped him; for in Bœotia (Hesychius) as in Attica (Pausanias, xxxi, 4) and in Naxos (Athenæus, iii, 78), some part of him was native to the soil, and he was nowhere wholly Thracian."—*Gods of Greece*, p. 82. Mr. Dyer had probably not studied Mr. Frazer's book when this passage was written, but it shows the opinions of specialists who have not called in the aid of ethnology. That part of Dionysus which was "native to the soil" was not Greek; the Greeks were immigrants to the land they adorned as their home, and the Dionysus "native to the soil" was shaped by them into the Athenian Dionysus.

when the inhabitants were advised by their priests to pray to the gods for water; whereupon the water sprang up spontaneously in a meadow about a third of a mile above the river, in an estate now called Rydon, amply sufficient to supply the wants of the place, and at present adequate, even in a dry summer, to work three mills. A lamb, it is said, has ever since that time been sacrificed as a votive thank-offering at Whitsuntide in the manner before mentioned. The said water appears like a large pond, from which in rainy weather may be seen jets springing up some inches above the surface in many parts. It has ever had the name of "Fair Water."* It is noticeable that, while the custom here described does not present any very extraordinary features, the popular legend concerning its origin introduces two very important elements—namely, its reference to "heathen days" and the title of "sacrifice" ascribed to the killing of the lamb. The genealogy of this custom, then, promises to take us back to the era of heathen sacrifice of animals.

The first necessity in tracing the genealogy is to analyze the custom as it obtains in nineteenth-century Devonshire. The analysis gives the following results:

1. The decoration of the victim lamb with garlands.
2. The killing and roasting of the victim by villagers.
3. The place of the ceremony in the middle of the village.

---

* *Notes and Queries*, vii, 353.

4. The selling of the roasted flesh to the poor.

*x*. The traditional origin of the custom as a sacrifice for water.

It seems clear that between the fourth step of the analysis and the traditional origin there are some considerable lacunæ to be filled up which prevent us at present from numbering the last item. The more primitive elements of this custom have been worn down to vanishing point, the practice probably being considered but an old-fashioned and cumbrous method of relieving distressed parishioners before the poor law had otherwise provided for them. Another example from Devonshire fortunately overlaps this one, and permits the restoration of the lost elements, and the consequent carrying back of the genealogy.

At the village of Holne, situated on one of the spurs of Dartmoor, is a field of about two acres, the property of the parish, and called the Ploy Field. In the center of this field stands a granite pillar (Menhir) six or seven feet high. On May morning, before daybreak, the young men of the village used to assemble there, and then proceed to the moor, where they selected a ram lamb, and, after running it down, brought it in triumph to the Ploy Field, fastened it to the pillar, cut its throat, and then roasted it whole, skin, wool, etc. At midday a struggle took place, at the risk of cut hands, for a slice, it being supposed to confer luck for the ensuing year on the fortunate devourer. As an act of gallantry the young men sometimes fought their way through the crowd to get a slice for the chosen among the young women, all of whom, in their best dresses, attended the Ram Feast, as it was called. Dancing, wrestling, and other games, assisted by copious libations of cider during the afternoon, prolonged the festivity till midnight.*

Analyzing this example, and keeping to the notation of the first analysis, we have the following results:—

2. The killing and roasting of the victim ram by villagers.

3. The place of the ceremony, at a stone pillar in a field which is common property.

4. The struggle for pieces of raw flesh "at the risk of cut hands."

5. The time of the ceremony, before daybreak.

6. The luck conferred by the possession of a slice of the flesh.

7. The festivities attending the ceremony.

Thus, of the five elements in the King's Teignton custom, three are retained in the Holne custom, and three additional ones of importance are added.

I think we may conclude, first, that the Holne custom is a more primitive form of a common original from which both have descended; secondly, that we may strike out the "roasting" as an entirely civilized ele-

---

* *Notes and Queries*, 1st ser., vii, 353. Compare Robertson Smith, *Religion of the Semites*, p. 320, and Owen, *Notes on the Naga Tribes*, pp. 15–16, for some remarkable parallels to this Devonshire custom. I would also refer to Miss Burne's suggestive description of the bull sacrifice in her *Shropshire Folklore*, p. 475.

ment due to modern influences. The final form of the analysis might then be restored from the two fragmentary ones as follows:

1. The decoration of the victim with garlands.
2. The killing of the victim by the community.
3. The place of the ceremony, on lands belonging to the community, and at a stone pillar.
4. The struggle for pieces of flesh by members of the community.
5. The time of the ceremony, before daybreak.
6. The sacred power of the piece of flesh.
7. The festivities attending the ceremony.
8. The origin of the ceremony, as a sacrifice to the god of waters.

The obvious analogy this bears to the Indian type we are examining scarcely needs to be insisted on, and I shall leave it to take its place among the group of European parallels.

The special sanctity of the head of the sacrificed victim, so apparent in the Indian festival, appears in European paganism and folklore in several places.* The Longobards adorned a divinely honored goat's head.† A well-known passage in Tacitus, describing the sacred groves of the Germans, states that the heads of the animals hung on boughs of trees, or, as it is noted in another passage, "immolati diis equi abscissum caput."

* Compare Robertson Smith, *Religion of the Semites*, pp. 359, 362.

† Grimm, *Teutonic Myth*, p. 31.

Heathendom, says Grimm, seems to have practiced all sorts of magic by cutting off horses' heads and sticking them up,* and he quotes examples from Scandinavia, Germany, and Holland. Passing on to folklore, we find that the witches of Germany in the thirteenth century were accused of adoring a beast's head.† A fox's head was nailed to the stable door in some parts of Scotland to bar the entrance of witches.‡ Camden has noted a curious ceremony obtaining at St. Paul's Cathedral. "I have heard," he says, "that the stag which the family of Le Baud in Essex was bound to pay for certain lands used to be received at the steps of the church by the priests in their sacerdotal robes and with garlands of flowers on their heads"; and as a boy he saw a stag's head fixed on a spear and conveyed about within the church with great solemnity and sounds of horns.# At Hornchurch, in Essex, a singular ceremony is recorded. The lessee of the tithes supplies a boar's head, dressed, and garnished with bay-leaves. In the afternoon of Christmas Day it is carried in procession into the field adjoining the churchyard, where it is wrestled for.‖

These customs are also confirmed by the records of archæology. In the belfry of Elsdon Church, Northum-

---

* Grimm, *Teutonic Myth.* p. 659. † *Ibid*, p. 1065.

‡ Dalyell, *Darker Superstitions of Scotland*, p. 148.

\# *Britannia*, Holland's translation, p. 426.

‖ *Notes and Queries*, 1st Ser., v, 106; *Gentleman's Magazine Library — Manners and Customs*, p. 221. It is also curious to note that leaden horns are fastened over the east part of the church.

berland, were discovered in 1877 the skeletons of three horses' heads. They were in a small chamber, evidently formed to receive them, and the spot was the highest part of the church; they were piled one against the other in a triangular form, the jaws being uppermost.*

I will not do more than say that these items of folklore, following those which relate to the sacrifice of the animal, confirm the parallel which is being sought for between the living ceremonial of Indian festivals and the surviving peasant custom in European folklore, and I pass on from the victims of the sacrifice to the actors in the scene. All the latent savagery exhibited in the action of tearing the victim to pieces has been noted both in the Indian type and in its folklore parallels. One might be tempted, perhaps, to draw attention to the curious parallel which the use of the whip by the Pótraj of the Indian village bears to the gad-whip service at Caistor, in Lincolnshire, especially as the whip here used is bound round with pieces of that magic plant the rowan-tree, and by tradition is connected with the death of a human being.† But this analogy may be one of the accidents of comparative studies, inasmuch as it is not supported by cumulative or other confirmatory evidence. No such reason need detain us from considering the fact of women offering their vows at the festival in a nude condition, covered only with the leaves and boughs of trees, because it is easy to turn

---

* *Berwickshire Naturalists' Field Club*, ix, 510.

† *Arch. Journ.*, vi, 239.

to the folklore parallels to this custom, in Mr. Hartland's admirable study of the Godiva legend.

Every one knows this legend, which, together with all details as to date and earliest literary forms, is explained by Mr. Hartland.* I shall therefore turn to the essential points. The ride of the Lady Godiva naked through the streets of Coventry is the legend told to account for an annual procession among the municipal pageants of that town. The converse view, that the pageant arose out of the legend, is disproved by the facts. To meet this theory the legend would have to be founded upon a definite historical fact concerning only the place to which it relates, namely, Coventry. For this, as Mr. Hartland shows, there is absolutely no proof; and parallels exist in two other places, one in the shape of an annual procession, the other in the shape of a legend only. I pass over the many interesting traces of the legend in folktales which Mr. Hartland has so learnedly collected and commented upon, and proceed to notice the other examples in England.

The first occurs at Southam, a village not far from Coventry. "Very little is known about it now, save one singular fact—namely, that there were two Godivas in the cavalcade, and one of them was black."† The

* *Science of Fairy Tales*, p. 71 *et seq.*

† Hartland, *op. cit.*, p. 85. This important discovery of Mr. Hartland's may fairly be compared with the "dirty practice of the Greeks" in the Dionysian mysteries noted above, a counterpart of which Mr. Lang some years ago could not find in modern folklore. —*Folklore Record*, ii, introd., p. ii.

second occurs at St. Briavels, in Gloucestershire. Here the privilege of cutting and taking the wood in Hudnolls, and the custom of distributing yearly upon Whitsunday pieces of bread and cheese to the congregation at church, are connected by tradition with a right obtained of some Earl of Hereford, then lord of the forest of Dean, at the instance of his lady, "upon the same hard terms that Lady Godiva obtained the privilege for the citizens of Coventry." *

Thus, then, we have as the basis for considering these singular survivals:

(*a*) The Coventry legend and ceremony, kept up as municipal custom, and recorded as early as the thirteenth century by Roger of Wendover.

(*b*) The Southam ceremony, kept up as local custom, unaccompanied by any legend as to origin.

(*c*) The St. Briavels legend, not recorded until toward the end of the eighteenth century, and accompanied by a totally different custom.

This variation in the local methods of keeping up this remarkable survival is one of some significance in the consideration of its origin,† and I now go on to compare it with an early ceremony in Britain, as noted by Pliny: "Both matrons and girls," says this authority, "among the people of Britain are in the habit of stain-

---

* Rudder, *History of Gloucestershire*, 1779, p. 307; Gomme, *Gentleman's Magazine Library—Manners and Customs*, p. 230; Hartland, *op. cit.*, p. 78.

† *Folklore*, i, 12.

ing their body all over with woad when taking part in the performance of certain sacred rites; rivaling thereby the swarthy hue of the Ethiopians, they go in a state of nature."* Between the customs and legends of modern folklore and the ancient practice of the Britons there is intimate connection, and the parallel thus afforded to the Indian festival seems complete. The attendance of votaries at a religious festival in a state of nudity has also been kept up in another form. At Stirling, on one of the early days of May, boys of ten and twelve years old divest themselves of clothing, and in a state of nudity run round certain natural or artificial circles. Formerly the rounded summit of Demyat, an eminence in the Ochil range, was a favorite scene of this strange pastime, but for many years it has been performed at the King's Knot in Stirling, an octagonal mound in the Royal gardens. The performances are not infrequently repeated at Midsummer and Lammas.† The fact that in this instance the practice is continued only by "boys of ten and twelve years old" shows that we have here one of the last stages of an old rite before its final abolition. It would have been difficult, perhaps, to attach much importance to this example as a survival of a rude prehistoric cult unless we had previously discussed the Godiva forms of it. But any one acquainted with the

* *Nat. Hist.*, lib. xxii, cap. 1. I think the passage in the poem of Dionysius Periegeta about the rites of the Amnites may be compared, the women being "decked in the dark-leaved ivy's clustering buds." See *Mon. Hist. Brit.*, p. xvii.

† Rogers, *Social Life in Scotland*, iii, 240.

frequent change of *personnel* in the execution of ceremonies sanctioned only by the force of local tradition will have little difficulty in conceding that the Scottish custom has a place in the series of folklore items which connects the Godiva ceremony with the religious rites of the ancient Britons as recorded by Pliny, thus cementing the close parallel which the whole bears to the Indian village festival.

I think it will be admitted that these parallels are sufficiently obvious to suggest that they tell the same story both in India and Europe. They do not, by actual proof, belong to the Aryans of India; they do not, therefore, by legitimate conclusion, belong to the Aryans of Europe.

But it may be argued that customs which in India are parts of one whole can not be compared with customs in Europe which are often isolated and sometimes associated with other customs. The argument will not hold good if the conditions of survivals in folklore already set forth are duly considered. But it can be met by the test of evidence. Some of the customs which in south India form a part of the festival of the village goddess are in other parts of India and in other countries independent customs, or associated with other surroundings altogether, thus substantiating my suggestion that this village festival of India has been welded together by the influence of races antagonistic to each other, which have been compelled to live together side by side for a long period.

## CHAPTER III.

### THE MYTHIC INFLUENCE OF A CONQUERED RACE.

It appears, then, that the influence of a conquered race does not die out so soon as the conquerors are established. Their religious customs and ritual are still observed under the new *régime*, and in some cases, as in India, very little, if any attempt is made to disguise their indigenous origin. Another influence exerted by the conquered over the conquerors is more subtle. It is not the adoption or extension of existing customs and beliefs, or the evolution of a new stage in custom and belief in consequence of the amalgamation. It is the creation of an entirely new influence, based on the fear which the conquered have succeeded in creating in the minds of the conquerors.

Has any one attempted to realize the effects of a permanent residence of a civilized people amidst a lower civilization, the members of which are cruel, crafty, and unscrupulous? In some regions of fiction, such as Kingsley's "Hereward" and Lytton's "Harold," a sort of picture has been drawn—a picture drawn and colored, however, in times far separated from those which witnessed the events. Fenimore Cooper has attempted the task with better materials in his stories of the white man and his relations to the red Indians. But by far the truest accounts are to be found in the dry records of official history. One such record has been transferred to the archives of the Anthropological Institute,* and it would be described by any ordinary reader as a record of the doings of demons.

Of course this phraseology is figurative. But figures of speech very often survive from the figures of the ancient mythic conceptions of actual events, and though we should simply style the doings of the Tasmanians fighting against the whites demoniacal as an appropriate figure of speech, people of a lower culture, and our own peasantry a few years back, would believe them to be demoniacal in the literal sense of that term. No one will doubt that there is much in savage warfare to suggest these ideas, and when it is remembered that savage warfare is waged by one tribe against another simply because they are strangers to each other—that not to be a member of a tribe is to be an enemy—it will not be surprising that the condition of hostility has produced its share of superstition.

It is the hostility between races, not the hostility between tribes of the same race, that has produced the most marked form of superstition; and it may be put down as one of the axioms of our science that the hostility of races wherever they dwell long together in close

* *Journ. Anthrop. Inst.*, iii., 9; *cf.* Nilsson's *Primitive Inhabitants of Scandinavia*, p. 176.

contact has always produced superstition. Unfortunately no examples of this have been noted by travelers as a general rule, but there is ample evidence in support of the statement, and I shall adduce some.

The inland tribes of New Guinea are distinct from those of the coast,* but the spirit beliefs of the coast tribes which are described as being unusually prevalent are chiefly derived from their fear of the aboriginal tribes. They believe, says Mr. Lawes, when the natives are in the neighborhood that the whole plain is full of spirits who come with them; all calamities are attributed to the power and malice of these evil spirits; drought, famine, storm and flood, disease and death, are all supposed to be brought by Vata and his hosts.† In this case the aborigines are represented as accompanied by their own spiritual guardians, who wage war upon the new-comers. In other cases aboriginal people are credited with the power of exercising demon functions or assuming demon forms. Thus every tribe in Western Australia holds those to the north of it in especial dread, imputing to them an immense power of enchantment; and this, says Mr. Oldfield, seems to justify the inference that the peopling of New Holland has taken place from various points toward the north.‡ The Hova tribes of Madagascar deified the Vazimba aborigines, and still consider their tombs as the most sacred

* Romilly, *From my Veranda*, p. 249.

† *Trans. Geog. Soc.*, N. S., ii, 615.

‡ *Trans. Ethnol. Soc.*, N. S., iii, 216, 235, 236.

objects in the country. These spirits are supposed to be of two kinds—the kindly disposed and the fierce and cruel. Some are said to inhabit the water, while others are terrestrial in their habits, and they are believed to appear to those who seek their aid in dreams, warning them and directing them.* In the case of the Ainos, the supposed aborigines of Japan, the subject and object of the superstition seem to be reversed, for it is the Ainos who are superstitiously afraid of the Japanese; † but it is to be observed that the ethnology of the Ainos, and their place in the country prior to the present condition of things, have not been sufficiently examined. Certainly their position in this group of superstitions will need consideration. Two examples may be mentioned of the attitude of Malays to their conquered foes. To a Malay an aboriginal Jakun is a supernatural being endowed with a supernatural power and with an unlimited knowledge of the secrets of nature; he must be skilled in divination, sorcery, and fascination, and able to do either evil or good according to his pleasure; his blessing will be followed by the most fortunate success, and his curse by the most dreadful consequences. When he hates some person he turns himself toward the house, strikes two sticks one upon the other, and, whatever may be the distance, his enemy will fall sick and

* *Anthrop. Inst.*, v, 190; Sibree, *Madagascar*, p. 135; Ellis, *Madagascar*, i, 123, 423.

† *Trans. Ethnol. Soc.*, N. S., vii, 24. Mr. Bickmore in this paper makes some very pertinent suggestions as to the probable ethnic origin of the Ainos.

even die if he perseveres in that exercise for a few days. Besides, to a Malay the Jakun is a man who by his nature must necessarily know all the properties of every plant, and consequently must be a clever physician, and the Malay when sick will obtain his assistance, or at least get some medicinal plants from him. The Jakun is also gifted with the power of charming the wild beasts, even the most ferocious.* The second example includes the Chinese. The Malays and Chinese of Malacca have implicit faith in the supernatural power of the Poyangs, and believe that many others among the aborigines are imbued with it. Hence they are careful to avoid offending them in any way, because it is believed they take offense deeply to heart, and will sooner or later, by occult means, revenge themselves. The Malays resort to them for the cure of diseases. Revenge also not infrequently sends them to the Poyangs, whose power they invoke to cause disease and other misfortune, or even death, to those who have injured them.† The Burmese and Siamese hold the hill tribes, the Lawas, in great dread, believing them to be man-bears.‡ The Budas of Abyssinia are looked upon as sorcerers and werewolves.#

These examples will serve to show the influences at work for the production of superstitious beliefs arising

* *Journ. Ind. Arch.*, ii, 273-274. † *Ibid.*, i, 328.

‡ Colquhoun's *Amongst the Shans*, p. 52; Bastian, *Œstl. Asien.*, i, 119.

# Hall's *Life of Nathaniel Pearce*, i, 286.

out of the hostility of races. My next point is to illustrate this principle in connection with the Aryan race. Do they, like the inferior races, endow with superhuman faculties the non-Aryan aborigines against whom they have fought in every land where they have become masters?

Again, we must turn to India for an answer to our question. The mountain ranges and great jungle tracts of southern India, says Mr. Walhouse, are inhabited by semi-savage tribes, who, there is good reason to believe, once held the fertile open plains, and were the builders of those megalithic sepulchres which abound over the cultivated country.* All these races are regarded by their Hindu masters with boundless contempt, and held unspeakably unclean. Yet there are many curious rights and privileges which the despised castes possess and tenaciously retain. Some of these in connection with the village festival, which has been examined at length, we already know. On certain days they may enter temples which at other times they must not approach; there are several important ceremonial and social observances which they are always called upon to inaugurate or take some share in, and which, indeed, says Mr. Walhouse, would be held incomplete and unlucky without them. But, what is more important for our immediate purpose, Mr. Walhouse also says that "the contempt and loathing in which they are ordinarily held are curiously

---

* *Journ. Anthrop. Inst.*, iv, 371.

tinctured with superstitious fear, for they are believed to possess secret powers of magic and witchcraft and influence with the old malignant deities of the soil who can direct good or evil fortune."* I lay stress upon this passage because in it is contained virtually the whole of the evidence I am seeking for. It is supported by abundant testimony, brought together with clearness and precision by Mr. Walhouse, and it is confirmed by many other authorities, whom it would be tedious to quote at length. To this day, says Colonel Dalton, the Aryans settled in Chota Nagpore and Singbhoom firmly believe that the Moondahs have powers as wizards and witches, and can transform themselves into tigers and other beasts of prey with a view to devouring their enemies, and that they can witch away the lives of man and beast.† The Hindus, Latham tells us, regard the Katodi with awe, believing that they can transform themselves into tigers.‡ I will finally quote the evidence from Ceylon. "The wild ignorant savages" who inhabited this island when the Hindus conquered it are termed by the chroniclers demons,# and demonism in Ceylon, originating with this non-Aryan aboriginal people, has grown into a cult.

---

* *Journ. Anthrop. Inst.*, iv, 371–372.

† *Trans. Ethnol. Soc.*, N. S., vi. 6; *Journ. As. Soc. Bengal*, 1866, part ii, 158. How these beliefs react on the non-Aryan races among themselves may be ascertained by referring to the Toda beliefs noted in *Trans. Ethnol. Soc.*, N. S., vii, 247, 277, 287.

‡ *Descriptive Ethnology*, ii, 457.

\# *Journ. As. Soc. Ceylon*, 1865–'66, p. 3; Tennent's *Ceylon*, i,

It bears on the question of the relationship between conquerors and conquered which has been illustrated by this evidence to observe that Professor Robertson Smith, from evidence apart from that I have used, has relegated demonism to the position of a cult hostile to and separate from the tribal beliefs of early people.*

I feel quite sure that the examples I have drawn from the history of savagery, and from the history of the conflict between Chinese and Hindu civilization and savagery, have already enabled the reader to detect many points of contact between these and the history of demonism and witchcraft in the Western world. I shall examine some of those points of contact, and then I shall turn to some more debatable matter.

The demonism of savagery is parallel to the witchcraft of civilization in the power which votaries of the two cults profess, and are allowed by their believers to possess, over the elements, over wild beasts, and in changing their own human form into some animal form, and it will be well to give some examples of these powers from the folklore of the British Isles.

(*a*) In Pembrokeshire there was a person, commonly known as "the cunning man of Pentregethen," who sold winds to the sailors, and who was reverenced in the

---

331. As to the remnants of these races, see Lassen, *Indische Alterthumskunde*, i, 199, 362.

* *Religion of the Semites*, pp. 55, 115, 129, 145, 246. Mr. Walhouse, in *Journ. Anthrop. Inst.*, v, 413, draws attention to the widespread and parallel beliefs in demons—beliefs which in India until lately, and in ancient Germany and Gaul altogether, were

neighborhood in which he dwelt much more than the divines; he could ascertain the state of absent friends, and performed all the wonderful actions ascribed to conjurers.* At Stromness, in the Orkneys, so late as 1814 there lived an old beldame who sold favorable winds to mariners. She boiled her kettle, muttered her incantations, and so raised the wind.† In the Isle of Man, Higden says, the women "selle to shipmen wynde, as it were closed under three knotes of threde, so that the more wynde he wold have, the more knotes he must vndo." ‡ At Kempoch Point, in the Firth of Clyde, is a columnar rock called the Kempoch Stane, from whence a saint was wont to dispense favorable winds to those who paid for them and unfavorable to those who did not put confidence in his powers; a tradition which seems to have been carried on by the Innerkip witches, who were tried in 1662, and some portions of which still linger among the sailors of Greenock.# These practices may be compared with the performances of the priestesses of Sena, who, as described by Pomponius Mela, were capable of rousing up the seas and winds by incantations. ‖

---

entirely ignored by inquirers, and he says they "belong to the Turanian races, and are antagonistic to the Aryan genius and feelings," p. 411. *Cf.* Tylor, *Primitive Culture*, i, 102.

* Howells's *Cambrian Superstitions*, 1831, p. 86.

† Gorrie, *Summers and Winters in Orkney*, p. 47.

‡ *Polychronicon* by Trevisa, i, cap. 44.

\# Cuthbert Bede, *Glencreggan*, i, 9, 44; *cf.* Sinclair's *Stat. Acc. of Scot.*, viii, 52.

‖ Pomponius Mela, iii, 8. It is curious to note that a district

(*b*) The power of witches over animals, and their capacity to transform themselves into animal shapes, is well known, though, as civilization has gradually eradicated the wilder sorts of animals, we do not now hear of these in connection with witchcraft. The most usual transformations are into cats and hares, and less frequently into red deer, and these have taken the place of wolves. Thus, cat transformations are found in Yorkshire; * hare transformations in Devonshire, Yorkshire, Wales, and Scotland; † deer transformations in Cumberland; ‡ raven transformations in Scotland; # cattle transformations in Ireland. ‖ Indeed the connection between witches and the lower animals is a very close one, and hardly anywhere in Europe does it occur that this connection is relegated to a subordinate place. Story after story, custom after custom, is recorded as appertaining to witchcraft, and animal transformation appears always.

From this it may be admitted that the general characteristics of the superstitions brought about by the contact between the Aryan conquerors of India and the non-Aryan aborigines are also represented in the cult of European witchcraft. When we pass from these general characteristics to some of the details, the identity

---

of Douglas in the Isle of Man is known as Sena.—*Trans. Manx Soc.*, v, 65: *Rev. Celt.*, x, 352.

* Henderson's *Folklore*, pp. 206, 207, 209.

† Henderson, pp. 201, 202, 208; Dalyell, *Darker Superstitions of Scotland*, p. 560; *Folklore*, ii, 291.

‡ Henderson, p. 204. # Dalyell, p. 559. ‖ *Ibid.*, p. 561.

of the Indian with the European superstitions is more emphatically marked. Thus, in Orissa it is believed that witches have the power of leaving their bodies and going about invisibly, but if the flower of the pân or betil-leaf can be obtained and placed in the right ear, it will enable the onlooker to see the witches and talk to them with impunity.* This is represented in folklore by the magic ointment, which enables people to see otherwise invisible fairies, and by the supposed property of the fern-seed, which makes people invisible.† Such a parallel as this could only have been produced by going back to origins. Again, in the charms resorted to by the demon-priests of Ceylon we find a close parallel, which belongs to the same category. A small image, made of wax or wood, or a figure drawn upon a leaf or something else, supposed to represent the person to be injured, is submitted to the sorcerer, together with a few hairs from the head of the victim, some clippings of his finger-nails, and a thread or two from a cloth worn by him. Nails made of a composition of five different kinds of metals, generally gold, silver, copper, tin, and lead are then driven into the image at all those points which represent the joints, the heart, the head, and other important parts of the body. The name of the intended victim being marked on the image, it is buried in the ground in some suitable place where the victim is likely

* *Handbook of Folklore*, p. 40.

† Hartland, *Science of Fairy Tales*, p. 59 *et seq.*; Brand, i, 315; *cf.* Grimm, *Teut. Myth.*, iii, 1210.

to pass over it.* This method of destruction by images is one of the most generally known among the practices of witchcraft in Europe. Plato alludes to it as obtaining among the Greeks of his period.† Boethius says a waxen image was fabricated for the destruction of one of the Scottish kings of the tenth century, and if this author is not to be taken too seriously for so early a period, his narrative is too circumstantial not to be readily accepted as a current belief at least of his own time.‡ The later Scottish practices contain all the elements of the Ceylon practices. The image was fabricated of any available materials, it was baptized by the name of the victim, or characterized by certain definitions identifying the resemblance, the various parts were pierced with pins or needles, or the whole was wasted by heat, and pieces of the victim's hair were associated with it.# These close parallels can not be accidental, and I am tempted to add that when we come upon other parallels which almost suggest the element of accident for their production, they may, after all, be due to parallel developments from the same originals.‖

* *Journ. As. Soc. Ceylon*, 1865–'66, p. 71; *cf.* Ward, *Hist. of the Hindoos*, ii, 100.

† Plato, *Laws*, lib. xi.

‡ Dalyell, *Darker Superstitions of Scotland*, pp. 332, 333.

# Dalyell, *op. cit.*, pp. 334–351.

‖ Such, for instance, as the revenge perpetrated upon the young wife in stopping the birth of her first child when her marriage was resented by a former financée of her husband; for which compare really remarkable parallels in *Ceylon As. Soc.*, 1865–'66, p. 70, and *Folklore Record*, ii, 116–117. It is important to note

It seems to me to be as impossible to ignore the evidence produced by these close parallels as to accept it at less than its full value. If the demonism of India is non-Aryan in origin and produced by the contact between Aryans and aborigines, the witchcraft of Europe must be equally non-Aryan in origin, and produced by the contact between Aryans and aborigines, even although during the ages of civilization the people who have carried on the cult have not kept up their race distinction side by side with their race superstition.*

Fortunately there is one singular fact preserved among the ceremonies of witchcraft in Scotland, which helps us to carry this argument a step forward toward absolute proof. In order to injure the waxen image of the intended victim, the implements used in some cases by the witches were stone arrowheads, or elf-shots, as they were called,† and their use was accompanied by an incantation.‡ Here we have, in the undoubted form of a prehistoric implement, the oldest untouched detail of early life which has been preserved by witchcraft, and it is such untouched oldest fragments, not their modern substitutions or additions, which must be accentuated

---

that Grimm rejects the idea of plagiarism to account for the similarity in witch-doings.—*Teut. Myth.*, iii. 1044.

* This observation even may have to be modified by further research, for in the Anglo-Saxon laws witchcraft is generally mentioned as a crime peculiar to serfs.

† Pitcairn, *Criminal Trials*, i, 192; Dalyell, *Darker Superstitions of Scotland*, pp. 352, 353; *cf.* Nilsson's *Primitive Inhabitants of Scandinavia*, p. 199.

‡ Dalyell, *op. cit.*, p. 357.

by the student of folklore; they clearly must be the starting-point of any explanation which may be sought for of the usages and superstitions of which they form a part. Grimm has stripped witchcraft of the accretions due to the action of the Church against heretics, and perceives "in the whole witch business a clear connection with the sacrifices and spirit world of the ancient Germans," * and it seems that this definition must be enlarged to include all branches of the Aryan race.

It is interesting to turn from these stone implements used in witchcraft to the beliefs about them in peasant thought. Irish peasants wear flint arrowheads about their necks set in silver as an amulet against elf-shooting.† In the west of Ireland, but especially in the Arran Isles, Galway Bay, they are looked on with great superstition. They are supposed to be fairy darts or arrows, which have been thrown by fairies, either in fights among themselves or at a mortal man or beast. The finder of one should carefully put it in a hole in a wall or ditch. It should not be brought into a house or given to any one; but the islanders of Arran are very fond of making votive offerings of them at the holy wells on the main-land. They carry them to the different patrons and leave them there, but they do not seem to leave them at the holy wells on the island.‡

---

* *Teut. Myth.*, iii, 1045.

† Henderson, *Folklore of Northern Countries*, p. 185.

‡ *Folklore Record*, iv, 112; *cf.* Vallancey, *Collectanea*, xiii; *Nenia Britannica*, p. 154.

If a quotation from the Brontës' eminently local novels is to be admitted as evidence, the belief that stone arrowheads were elf-shots was prevalent in Yorkshire.*

In Scotland, Edward Lhwyd noted in 1713 that "the most curious as well as the vulgar throughout this country are satisfied they often drop out of the air, being shot by fairies," and that "they have not been used as amulets above thirty or forty years." † At Lauder and in Banffshire the peasantry called them elf-arrowheads.‡ At Wick, in Caithness, the peasantry asserted that they were fairies' arrows, and that the fairies shot them at cattle, which instantly fell down dead, though the hide of the animal remained quite entire.# That this was a Lowland Scotch belief is also attested by Keightley's collection of facts.‖

Thus, then, in witchcraft and in peasant thought there is a common belief as to prehistoric arrowheads having belonged to beings known as elves. It proves, as Nilsson observes, that it was not the Celts themselves, but a people considered by them to be versed in magic, who fabricated and used these stone arrows.^ These people, whoever they may prove to be, were therefore powerful enough to introduce mythic conceptions con-

* *Folklore Journal*, i, 300.

† *Folklore Record*, iv, 169; *cf.* Gregor's *Folklore of Northeast of Scotland*, p. 59.

‡ Sinclair's *Stat. Acc. Scot.* i, 73; iii, 56,

# *Ibid.*, x, 15; xxi, 148. ‖ *Fairy Mythology*, pp. 351, 352.

^ *Primitive Inhabitants of Scandinavia*, p. 200.

cerning themselves into the minds of their conquerors, and some authorities of eminence have not hesitated to urge that they have even left traditions of their existence in a more historical shape.* "Who," asks Mr. Campbell, "were these powers of evil who can not resist iron—these fairies who shoot *stone* arrows, and are of the foes to the human race? Is all this but a dim, hazy recollection of war between a people who had iron weapons and a race who had not—a race whose remains are found all over Europe?" †

We are here met by two opposing theories—one whose upholders look back upon the fairy traditions as evidence of so much actual history, the other as evidence only of the spirit beliefs of past ages.

But if the close inter-relationship between fairy-beliefs and witch-beliefs be steadily kept in mind, these opposing theories may, I think, be brought into something like unison. Mr. Hartland has proved this close inter-relationship by a lengthy investigation, ‡ and it

---

* Skene, in the first volume of his *Celtic Scotland*, and Elton, in his *Origins of English History*. cap. vii, are the most available authorities on this subject.

† *Tales of the West Highlands*, p. lxxvi; Nilsson, in *Primitive Inhabitants of Scandinavia* (p. 247 *et seq.*), and MacRitchie, in his *Testimony of Tradition*, have followed this line of argument.

‡ *Science of Fairy Tales, passim.* Grimm's observation that the witches' devils have proper names so strikingly similar in formation to those of elves and kobolds that one can scarcely think otherwise than that nearly all devils' names of that class are descended from other folk-names for those sprites—*Teut. Myth.*, iii, 1063—strikingly confirms the explanation I have ventured upon as to the connection between witchcraft and fairycraft.

must henceforth be the basis of research into these departments of folklore.

We commence the task of certifying to the unison of these two theories with the fact of the personal element in witchcraft—the attribution of magical powers, derived from the spirit of evil, to certain definite classes of people, the acceptance of this attribution by the people concerned, and their claim to have become acquainted with their supposed powers by initiation. I am inclined to lay great stress upon the act of initiation. It emphasizes the idea of a caste distinct from the general populace, and it postulates the existence of this caste anterior to the time when those who practice their supposed powers first come into notice. Carrying back this act of initiation age after age, as the dismal records of witchcraft enable us to do for some centuries, it is clear that the people from time to time thus introduced into the witch caste carried on the practices and assumed the functions of the caste even though they came to it as novices and strangers. We thus arrive at an artificial means of descent of a particular group of superstitions, and it might be termed initiatory descent.

But descent by initiation was not invented without some good and sufficient cause, and this cause will be found, I think, in the failure of blood-descent. In the primitive Aryan family failure of blood-descent led to the legal fiction of adoption, and the history of caste almost everywhere shows the same phenomenon. I do not wish to ask too much from this argument before it is substantiated by evidence, but that we may take it as a sound working hypothesis is confirmed by the fact that it supplies the missing link in a most important series of developments clearly marked in the history of witchcraft and its connection with fairycraft.

The only people occupying the lands of modern European civilization who have not succeeded in marking their descendants with the stamp of their race origin are the non-Aryans. Celt, Teuton, Scandinavian, and Slav are still to be found in centers definable on the map of Europe, but except in the Basque Pyrenees the forerunners of the Aryan peoples have become absorbed by their conquerors. Blood-descent was of no avail to them for the keeping alive of their old faiths and beliefs. That they resorted to initiation as a remedy is the suggestion I wish to make, and that in witchcraft there has been preserved some of the non-Aryan faiths and beliefs is the conclusion I wish to draw—a conclusion which is met more than half-way by the close parallel which, as we have already partly seen, exists between the beliefs and practices of witches and non-Aryan beliefs.

I think it is more than probable that the ancient cult of Druidism will prove to be a factor in the race history of witchcraft. At the time when all traces of Druidism, as such, had completely died out in Britain, some of the practices attributed to witches were exact reproductions of the practices attributed to Druids by the earlier writers. One of the most significant, as it is one of the most painful, of these practices has for its basis the belief that the life of one man could only be redeemed by that of another. The evidence for the Druidical side of this parallel is given by Cæsar and other authorities. The evidence for it in witchcraft is given in some of the seventeenth-century trials, where all the details of the horrid rites are related with minute accuracy.* I shall have occasion to refer to these details at some length later on, but I note here that they supply us not only with evidence of the continuity in witchcraft of a particular Druidic belief, but also of the continuity of the methods of adapting this belief to practice—namely, through the interposition of a trained adept, in fact the priestess of a cult; for in this instance, at all events, the Scottish witch is the successor of the Druid priestess. She is so in other characteristics already noted—in her capacity for transformation into animal form, in her power over winds and waves, both being common to witch and Druidess alike.

It is no answer to the argument that Druidism was continued by witchcraft to point to the apparent chronological gap between the decline of one and the earliest historical mention of the other.† That Druidism con-

* *Cf.* Forbes Leslie, *Early Races of Scotland*, i, 83; Dalyell, *Darker Superstitions of Scotland*, p. 176.

† Grimm says that the earlier middle ages had known of magicians and witches only in the milder senses. as legendary elvish beings peopling the domain of vulgar belief, or even as demoniacs.—*Teut. Myth.*, iii, 1067.

tinued to exist long after it was officially dead, can be proved. The character of much of the paganism of the early Scots and Picts has been accepted as Druidic by Mr. Skene. The histories of the labors of St. Patrick and St. Columba abound in references to the Druids. "The Druids of Laogaire," says an ancient poem, "concealed not from him the coming of Patrick."* Columba competes with the Druids in his supernatural powers on behalf of Christianity.† Druidism thus came into contact with Christianity. Mr. Skene and Mr. O'Curry, however, are inclined to think that at this time it was not the Druidism of Cæsar and Pliny—"it was," says the former writer, "a sort of fetichism, which peopled all the objects of nature with malignant beings to whose agency its phenomena were attributed."‡ Mr. O'Curry gives some of the vast number of allusions to the Druids in Irish MSS., which contain instances of contests in Druidical spells, of clouds raised by incantations of Druidesses, of the interpretation of dreams, of the raising of tempests, of the use of a yew wand instead of oak or mistletoe, of auguries drawn from birds, and other peculiar rites and beliefs; but he distinctly repudiates the idea that Irish Druidism, as made known by the MSS., was like the classical Druidism in its adoption of human sacrifice,

---

* Stokes's *Gaedelica*, p. 131.

† Skene, *Celtic Scotland*, ii, 115–117, gives the principal evidence under this head. *Cf.* Elton, *Origins of English History*, pp. 273–274.

‡ Skene, *Celtic Scotland*, ii, 118.

or in its priests being servants of any special positive worship.*

It is difficult to contest opinions like these, but they do not appear to be borne out by the facts. For instance, on the question of human sacrifice the *Book of Ballymote* tells us how one of the kings brought fifty hostages from Munster, and, dying before he reached his palace, the hostages were buried alive around the grave.† The evidence of Scottish witchcraft, already quoted, is clear as to the sacrifice of one human being for another in case of sickness; and Mr. Elton says that the Welsh and Irish traditions contain many traces of the custom of human sacrifice. "Some of the penalties of the ancient laws," he says, "seemed to have originated in an age when the criminal was offered to the gods; the thief and the seducer of women were burned on a pile of logs or cast into a fiery furnace; the maiden who forgot her duty was burned, or drowned, or sent adrift to sea." ‡ To these examples must be added the well-known story of Vortigern, who, on the recommendation of the British Druids, sought for a victim to sacri-

---

* O'Curry, *Manners and Customs of the Irish*, ii, 222–228.

† O'Curry, p. cccxx; *cf.* Elton, *Origins of English History*, p. 272.

‡ *Origins of English History*, p. 271. Rhys, *Celtic Heathendom*, p. 224, says: "Irish Druidism absorbed a certain amount of Christianity, and it would be a problem of considerable difficulty to fix on the point where it ceased to be Druidism, and from which onward it could be said to be Christianity in any restricted sense of that term."

fice at the foundation of his castle;* the parallel sacrifice of St. Oran in Iona by Columba;† and the sacrifice of the first-born of children and flocks, in order to secure power and peace in all their tribes and to obtain milk and corn for the support of their families.‡

These facts are perhaps sufficient to show that the evidence for the continuity of Druidism, whatever Druidism may have been, meets the other evidence as to the presence in witchcraft of Druid beliefs and practices sufficiently nearly in point of time for it to be a reasonable argument to affirm that witchcraft is the lineal successor of Druidism. The one point necessary, then, to complete the argument I have advanced is, that Druidism must be identified as a non-Aryan cult. I am aware that this point still awaits much investigation by Celtic philologists and historians, but in the mean time I am content to claim that considerable weight must be given to Professor Rhys's twice-repeated affirmation that his researches go to prove Druidism to be of non-Aryan origin,# especially as his researches lie in quite a different direction to my own.

---

* *Irish Nennius*, cap. 40. O'Curry mentions this as evidence for the differentiation of Irish and British Druidism.—*Manners and Customs*, ii, 222.

† Stokes's *Three Middle Irish Homilies*, p. 119; *Rev. Celt.*, ii, 200; *Stat. Acc. of Scotland*, vii, 321; Pennant's *Tour*, ii, 298.

‡ *Book of Leinster*, quoted by Rhys, *Hibbert Lectures*, p. 201.

\# Rhys, *Celtic Britain*, pp. 67-75; *Lectures on Welsh Philology*, p. 32; compare *Celtic Heathendom*, p. 216 *et seq.*; I have dealt with the institutional side of Druidism in its non-Aryan origin in my *Village Community*, p. 104 *et seq.*

Whether, therefore, we rest our argument upon the parallels to be found between witch practices and beliefs and non-Aryan practices and beliefs, or upon the hypothesis that the initiation necessary to the performance of witchcraft is in reality the method of continuing Druidic beliefs and practices when the possibilities of continuing them by race descent had died out, there is proof enough that in witchcraft is contained the survival of non-Aryan practices and beliefs—practices and beliefs, that is, which the non-Aryan peoples possessed concerning themselves and their own powers.

We next have to meet the question as to the race origin of fairy beliefs, in so far as they are parallel to witch beliefs. If witchcraft represents ancient aboriginal belief in direct descent by the channels just examined, what part of the same aboriginal belief does fairycraft represent, and how is its separation from witchcraft to be accounted for?

The theory that fairies are the traditional representatives of an ancient pygmy race has met with considerable support from folklorists. It is needless to repeat all the arguments in support of this theory which have been advanced during the past twenty years, because they are contained in works easily accessible and well known. But it is important to note that these beliefs must have originated not with the aboriginal pygmy race themselves, but with the conquering race who overpowered them and drove them to the hills and out-parts of the land. The influence of the despised, out-driven aborigines did not cease after the conflict was over. It produced upon the minds of their conquerors mythic conceptions, which have during the lapse of time become stereotyped into certain well-defined lines of fairy lore.

At this point we may discuss how the parallel between witchcraft and fairycraft is explained by the ethnological characteristics which have been advanced. Witchcraft has been explained as the survival of aboriginal beliefs from aboriginal sources. Fairycraft has been explained as the survival of beliefs about the aborigines from Aryan sources. The aborigines, as is proved from Indian and other evidence, not only believed in their own demoniacal powers, but sought in every way to spread this belief among their conquerors. Thus, then, the belief of the aborigines about themselves, and of the conquering race about the aborigines, would be on all material points identical; and by interpreting the essentials of witchcraft and of fairycraft as the survivals in folklore of the mythic influence of a conquered race upon their conquerors, we are supported by the facts which meet us everywhere in folklore, and by an explanation which alone is adequate to account for all the phenomena. It has been held, indeed, by Grimm and others, that witchcraft is a direct offshoot from fairy beliefs, consequent upon the action of the Christian Church in stamping fairydom with a connection with the devil. But if this argument is worth anything, it would account for the fact that fairydom, after throwing off such a powerful offshoot as witchcraft, should have itself continued in undiminished force with all the old beliefs attached to it. But it does not account for this difficulty. On the other hand, the explanation I have attempted is not involved with such a difficulty. The various phenomena fit into their places with remarkable precision; there is no twisting of any of the details, and not only analogies but differences are accounted for.

I am tempted to put this argument into genealogical form, to show more clearly the lines along which we have traveled It would be set forth as follows:

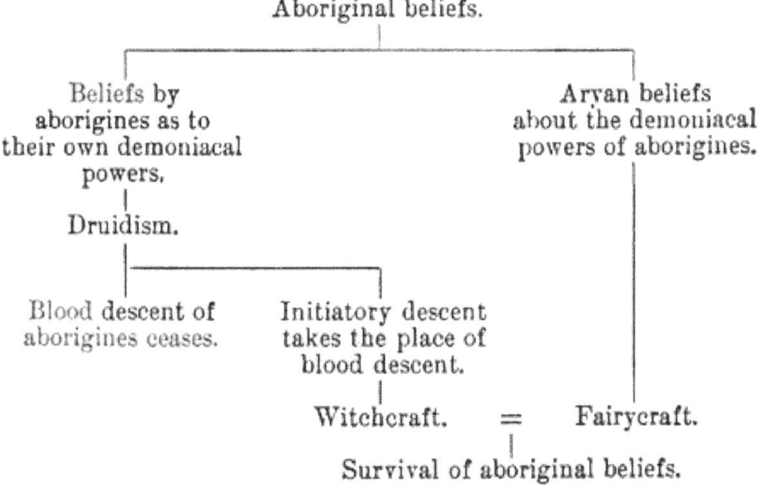


I do not suggest that this table should be hardened into an absolute rule. All that it is intended for, and all that folklore can attempt at present, is to indicate some of the results which may be attained by a close and systematic study of its details. These details in some departments will allow of something like precision in their arrangement; in others we must still grope about for some time to come yet. But if we attempt precision in arrangement, we must be careful not to allow it to become the means of detaching any items of folklore from their proper place amid all the other items. Their relationship to each other is, indeed, the only means by which we may trace out their origins. The neglect of this principle in connection with the numerous accounts of the higher divinities both of classical and modern times, has helped to bring about the idea that in Europe both higher and lower divinities belong to the same people.

# CHAPTER IV.

## THE LOCALIZATION OF PRIMITIVE BELIEF.

IT would seem that we may distinguish in the prehistoric ages of man certain data which point to a pretribal society. The argument as it stands at present is not one to insist upon with too much precision, either with reference to its illustration of earliest man, or with reference to its influence on later man. Rather, it must be continually borne in mind that the evolution of society does in some measure point back to an early phase of extreme localization, and that biological evidence strongly supports such a view. So far as the survey of primitive belief has proceeded with reference to the origin of certain of its classes, there seems to be some proof of the same course of evolution. Thus Dormer says: "If monotheism had been an original doctrine, traces of such a belief would have remained among all peoples; if the cure of disease by medication had been the original method, such a useful art would never have been so utterly lost that sorcery should wholly usurp its place; in savage animism we find no survivals which show inconsistencies with it." * But savage animism is

* Dormer, *Origin of Primitive Superstitions*, pp. 386, 387.

founded upon, and essentially bound up with, locality. One word only is required in proof of this, and for this purpose we naturally turn to Dr. Tylor. Studying his careful analysis of animism, and the evidence brought forward to support it, it appears clear enough that the emphasis of animism lies in its localization—"the local spirits which belong to mountain and rock and valley, to well and stream and lake—in brief, to those natural objects which in early ages aroused the savage mind to mythological ideas." *

I take it to be a distinct advance in culture when mankind began to separate himself from local worship. In the study of Semitic religions which Professor Robertson Smith has given us, he has touched upon this point in a chapter which contains many valuable suggestions, but he does not appear to me to mark sufficient distinction between the tribal gods which are, according to his evidence, tending to become local, and the primitive local gods of the land which had never become tribal.† The distinction is an important one, and has a definite bearing upon the ethnology of Semitic ritual. It must, however, be approached from the savage side. No one has paid closer attention to this than Major Eilis in his studies of African beliefs, and it seems clear from these that the transition is from local to tribal, and not *vice versa*. "The deified powers in nature," says Major Ellis, "the rivers and lagoons, being

* Tylor, *Primitive Culture*, ii, 187.

† *Religion of the Semites*, cap. iii.

necessarily local, would in course of time, from at first being merely regarded as the gods of the district, come to be regarded as the gods of the people living in the district; in this way would probably arise the idea of national or tribal gods; so that eventually the gods, instead of being regarded as being interested in the whole of mankind, would come to be regarded as being interested in separate tribes or nations alone." * With some slight amendments, this passage fairly interprets the evidence from all parts of the savage world, and I have been gradually forced to the conviction that the greatest triumph of the Aryan race was its emancipation from the principle of local worship, and the rise of the conception of gods who could and did accompany the tribes wheresoever they traveled. No doubt tribal gods incline to become local once more—to have a fixed habitat, a sanctuary, a home made holy by the presence of the god. This is particularly the case with the Semitic gods, and its close approximation to the form of belief in purely local deities has prevented Professor Robertson Smith from entering upon a most interesting phase of Semitic ritual. But the gods of the Aryans have never been quite so local in their nature, even after long residence with their worshipers in much-loved homes. All the local haunts of the Greek gods do not make Greek gods local—they are still tribal gods, with a special local home for the time being.

It is not, perhaps, worth while pursuing this subject

* Ellis, *Tshi-speaking Peoples*, p. 114.

further on the general evidence. It would occupy much space for the point to be proved in detail, but there is already sufficient illustration of it in the text-books of anthropology to allow me to pass on to the special evidence I am in search of. Thus we find that Professor Rhys draws a line of distinction between the greater divinities of the Celtic pantheon, who lent themselves to localization, and the crowd of minor divinities who were never anything else than *genii locorum*. Among the latter he includes "the spirits of particular forests, mountain tops, rocks, lakes, rivers, river sources, and all springs of water which have in later times been treated as holy wells."* To these must be added all those agricultural deities, the ritual of whom has been examined so thoroughly by Mr. Frazer. Earth deities, claiming their sacrifice of human blood; tree deities, claiming the life of their priest; corn deities, whose death forms part of their own cult; rain deities, claiming victims for their service, form no part of any recognizable tribal cult, but are essentially the fixed heritage of the places where they originated and fructified.

This classification of the local deities leads up to an important point in the ethnology of folklore. Turning back to Professor Rhys's group, we find him saying of them that "it has been supposed, and not without reason, that these landscape divinities reacted powerfully on the popular imagination in which they had their existence by imparting to the physical surroundings of the

* *Celtic Heathendom*, p. 105.

Celt the charm of a weird and unformulated poetry. But what race was it that gave the Celtic landscape of antiquity its population of spirits? The Celtic invaders of Aryan stock brought their gods with them to the lands they conquered; but as to the innumerable divinities attached, so to say, to the soil, the great majority of them were very possibly the creations of the people here before the Celts." * I would interpret in the same way the agricultural deities which are not included in Professor Rhys's dictum. Without some such interpretation it is difficult to account for the savagery of the ritual practiced in their worship, or for its extensive and thoroughly settled forms. Reckoning from the Aryan occupation of eastern and northern Europe, there is no time for such a cult to have developed from the primitive pastoral worship of the Aryans, even if it is possible to assume, as it would be necessary to do, that pastoral life is an antecedent to agricultural life. Against such an assumption, though it has been urged by some distinguished scholars, I would enter the strongest protest. There is no proof of it in anthropological evidence. There is proof of pastoral tribes settling down, as the Aryans have done, as the overlords of aboriginal agriculturists; of the gradual extinction of pastoral life in the development of settled tribal life; of the final extinction of tribal life altogether in the rise of the village community. But all this is distinctly antagonistic to the idea that pastoral life is

* Rhys, *loc. cit.*

older and more primitive than agricultural. Connected with agricultural life we get the rudest tribes of savages, the rudest forms of culture. As Mr. Keary has said: "If the remains of fetichism could be so vital, fetichism itself must have had a lengthened sway; but the people could never have become the Aryan nation had their notions of unity been confined to the local fetich and the village commune."* Let us once clearly understand that the local fetichism to be found in Aryan countries simply represents the undying faiths of the older race, which the Aryans at last incorporated into their own higher beliefs, and the difficulties lying in the way of accounting for Aryan progress, which have been recognized but not met, seem to vanish.

The localization of primitive belief, then, is, as it seems to me, an important factor in the consideration of survivals. Given the natural object which originated, in the rude mind of early man, a set of beliefs, and the continued existence of the natural object would greatly assist the continued existence of the beliefs. River worship is a case in point. It is found almost everywhere among people of a rude or savage culture, and its origin is not far to seek. Thus among some African tribes "there are many deities bearing the name of Prah, all of whom are spirits of the river Prah, called by the natives Bohsŭm-Prah. At each town or considerable village upon its banks sacrifice is held on a day about the middle of October to Prah; and from the

* *Outlines of Primitive Belief*, p. 110.

fact of the one day being common to all the peoples dwelling on the river, and that the sacrificial ceremonies are the same throughout, it seems evident that originally this worship was established for one great deity of the river, although now the inhabitants of each village believe in the separate spirit of the Prah, who resides in some part of the river near their hamlet. Everywhere along the river the priests of these gods officiate in groups of three, two male and one female, an arrangement which is peculiar to Prah. . . . The usual sacrifice was two human adults, one male and one female. . . . Crocodiles are sacred to Prah." *

This is not far removed from the Esthonian belief. In Esthonia there is a particular stream which has long been the object of reverence—the Wohhanda. In the olden time no Esthonian would fell any tree that grew on its banks or break one of the reeds that fringed its watercourse. If he did he would die within the year. The brook, along with the spring that gave it birth, was purified periodically, and it was believed that if dirt was thrown into either, bad weather would be the result. Tradition speaks of offerings—sometimes of little children—having been made to Wohhanda; the river god being a little man in blue and yellow stockings, sometimes visible to mortal eye, resident in the stream and in the habit of occasionally rising out of it.†

People with beliefs like these do not readily give

* Ellis, *Tshi-speaking Peoples*, p. 64; *cf.* pp. 32, 33.

† Latham, *Descriptive Ethnology*, i, 418.

them up, because the power of the river to work harm does not die out as race succeeds race among the inhabitants of river districts. When in the Solomon Islands a man accidentally falls into the river and a shark attacks him, he is not allowed to escape. If he succeeds in eluding the shark, his fellow-tribesmen will throw him back to his doom, believing him to be marked out for sacrifice to the god of the river.* But this explanation exactly fits the superstition against rescuing a drowning person which is made so familiar to us by Scott's story *The Pirate.*† The form of the peasant belief may be thus given: "Among the seamen of Orkney and Shetland it was deemed unlucky to rescue persons from drowning, since it was held as a matter of religious faith that the sea is entitled to certain victims, and if deprived would avenge itself on those who interfere."‡

I will now turn to some examples of river worship in Great Britain. The existence of water spirits is a well-known belief,# but I am desirous of noting rather the deities of special rivers. It is curious that in Scotland persons who bore the name of the river Tweed were supposed to have as an ancestor the *genie* of the river of that name.‖ The river Auld Gramdt, or Ugly Burn, in the county of Ross, springing from Loch Glaish, was

* Codrington, *The Melanesians*, p. 179.
† *Folklore Journal*, vii, 44; *ibid.*, iii, 185.
‡ Tudor's *Orkney and Shetland*, p. 176.
# Dalyell, *Darker Superstitions of Scotland*, p. 543.
‖ Rogers, *Social Life in Scotland*, iii, 336.

regarded with awe as the abode of the water-horse and other spiritual beings.* The river Spey is spoken of as "she," and it is a common belief that at least one victim is necessary every year.†

One of the principal English river divinities has been figured on a Roman pavement. This pavement is the well-known one at Lydney Park, Gloucestershire, on the western bank of the Severn, in the territory of the ancient Silures. Three inscriptions are preserved, as follows:

(1) DEVO NODENTI.
(2) D. M. NODONTI.
(3) DEO NUDENTE M.

and Professor Rhys has discussed their philological importance.‡

The remains of the temple at Lydney, for such it is generally considered, connects this god with the sea, or rather with the worship of water, and in this case with the river Severn in the following particulars. The mosaic floor displays representations of sea-serpents or the κήτεα accompanying Glaucus in the Greek mythology, and fishes supposed to stand for the salmon of the Severn; an ugly band of red surrounds the mouth of a funnel leading into the ground beneath, which hole is supposed to have been used for libations to the god. A small plaque of bronze found on the spot gives us probably a representation of the god himself. The principal

---

* Dalyell, *op. cit.*, p. 544. † *Folklore*, iii, 72.
‡ *Celtic Heathendom*, p. 126.

figure is a youthful deity crowned with rays like Phœbus and standing in a chariot drawn by four horses. On either side the winds are typified by a winged genius floating along, and the rest of the space is left to two tritons, while a detached piece, probably of the same bronze, represents another triton and a fisherman who has just succeeded in hooking a salmon.*

Of course this work is Roman, and must therefore bear the stamp of the Roman interpretation of the local god. It would be conventionalized to the Roman standard of the water god, Neptune. I do not at all consider that we have here the British embodiment of the god, but simply the Roman interpretation of the British belief—the description of the British cult in monumental records instead of in literary records.

We pass, however, from archæology to folklore. Professor Rhys identifies the epigraphical form of the Severn god's name, Nodens, with the Welsh Lludd and with the Irish Nuada. The first name brings us to the legendary King Lud, who is said to have built London, and whose name preserved in our Ludgate Hill is sufficient to attest the veracity of Geoffrey of Monmouth's record that one of the Welsh names for London was Caer Lûdd, or Lud's Fort. "The probability," says Professor Rhys, "that as a temple on a hill near the Severn associated him with that river in the west, so a

---

* I take this summary from Professor Rhys, *loc. cit.*; the whole find has been described in a separate volume, and profusely illustrated by the Rev. W. H. Bathurst and C. W. King.

still more ambitious temple on a hill connected him with the Thames in the east"—a probability which is confirmed by the tradition, so often quoted, that St. Paul's Cathedral has taken the place of a heathen temple.

The second name, the Irish Nuada, takes us to the Boyne, which was known as Righ Mná Nuadhat—that is, the wrist or forearm of Nuadhat's wife.* The identification of Nuada as a river god is clearly shown by the legend connected with the well of the Blessed Trinity at which the Boyne rises. One of the miraculous virtues of this well was that any one who approached it except the monarch and his three cup-bearers was instantly deprived of sight. Boan, the queen of Nuada, determined to test the mystical powers, and not only approached the well and defied its powers, but passed three times round it to the left, as was customary in incantations. Upon completion of the third round the waters rose, mutilated the daring queen, and as she fled to the sea, followed her until she reached the present mouth of the river. †

The river Dee, near Chester, was supposed to possess characteristics in the time of Giraldus Cambrensis which marks its godlike attributes. "The inhabitants

---

* O'Curry, *Manners and Customs of the Irish*, iii, 156.

† Wilde's *Beauties of the Boyne*, p. 24, from the *Book of Lecan* and the *Book of Ballymote*. Near the bridge at Stackallan a patron used to be held, and it was customary for the people to swim their cattle across the river at this spot as a charm against fairies and certain diseases.—Wilde, *loc. cit.*, p. 171. A similar legend is told of the Shannon.—O'Curry, *Manners and Customs*, ii, 143, 144; *cf. Rev. Celtique*, vi, 244.

of those parts assert that the waters of this river change their fords every month, and as it inclines more toward England or Wales they can with certainty prognosticate which nation will be successful or unfortunate during the year."* Professor Rhys draws attention to the name of another river—the Belisama—which marks it out as one that was formerly considered divine, the name occurring in inscriptions found in Gaul as that of the goddess equated with the Minerva of Italy.† If this river is to be identified with the Ribble, as Professor Rhys suggests, folklore has preserved something of the old cult. This river has a spirit called Peg o' Nell, and a spring in the grounds of Waddow bears her name and is graced by a stone image, now headless, which is said to represent her. A tradition connects this Peg o' Nell with an ill-used servant at Waddow Hall, who, in revenge for her mistress's successful malediction in causing her death, was inexorable in demanding every seven years a life to be quenched in the waters of the Ribble. "Peg's night" was the closing night of the septenniate, and when it came round, unless a bird, a cat, or a dog was drowned in the stream, some human being was certain to fall a victim there.‡ The river Tees has also a sprite, which is called Peg Powler, a sort of Lorelei, says

---

* Giraldus, *Itinerary through Wales*, ii, cap. xi; *cf. Rev. Celtique*, ii, 2–5, for the distribution of "Dee" as a river name and its mythological meaning.

† *Celtic Britain*, 2d edit., p. 68.

‡ Henderson, *Folklore of Northern Counties*, p. 265; Harland and Wilkinson's *Lancashire Folklore*, p. 89.

Henderson, with green tresses and an insatiable desire for human life. The foam or froth which is often seen floating on the higher portion of the Tees in large masses is called "Peg Powler's suds," and the finer, less sponge-like froth is called "Peg Powler's cream."* Childıen were still warned in Mr. Denham's days from playing on the banks of the river by threats that Peg Powler would drag them into the water.† The Yore, near Middleham, is said to be much infested with a horrid kelpie or water-horse, who rises from the stream at evening and ramps along the meadows searching for prey, and it is imagined that the kelpie claims at least one human victim annually.‡

These and the hill deities are essentially inimical to man, but the local deities resident in wells are friendly. Professor Robertson Smith has drawn from the Semitic facts sufficient general evidence of the rise of well or spring worship,# identifying it with the agricultural life of aborigines who had not yet developed the idea of a heavenly god. It will be for us to examine the evidence in a European country, and sufficient examples are to be found in the British Isles for the purpose.

It is not true of many forms of popular superstition, though it is frequently stated to be true, that they prevail universally through the country. But in the case of well worship it may be asserted with some confidence

* Henderson, p. 265. † *Denham Tracts.*

‡ Longstaffe, *Richmondshire*, p. 96; Barker's *Wensleydale*, p. 286. # *Religion of the Semites*, cap. iii; *cf.* p. 99.

that it prevails in every country of the three kingdoms, and this fact necessitates a very careful inquiry as to its origin. A purely local cult, like that connected with river worship, can be accounted for by appealing to its special character as a belief that crops up only here and there in isolation. The case is altogether different when dealing with a general cult everywhere prevalent. It might have originated with the incoming of any of the dominating forces of culture—with Christianity, with the Aryan conquest by Teuton and Celt. In fact, what we have first to reckon with in examining into its origin is its general prevalence. The question forms itself in the following way: Did such a worship originate from above and spread downward among the people until it became universal, or did it begin from the people and penetrate upward? Of course the question put in these terms does not indicate how important it is to endeavor to obtain an answer to it. But this is the first step, and we may presently translate it into more definite terms.

Of the antiquity of the custom we are assured by the well-known prohibitions of it by the Saxon clergy and by Canute, and this also certifies to its general prevalence, while its incorporation into the Roman Catholic ritual of Ireland * indicates that its influence

---

* No religious place in Ireland could be without a holy well. Otway, *Sketches in Erris*, p. 213; *cf. Proc. Roy. Hist. and Arch. Soc. Ireland*, 4th Ser., ii, 268, where the evidence on the subject is summarized very well. St. Columbkille is said to have "sained three hundred well-springs that were swift."—Whitley Stokes, *Three Middle Irish Homilies*.

has the capacity, at all events, to penetrate upward. A worship that was formally and officially prohibited in the tenth and eleventh centuries and has been formally accepted in modern times could not, under any circumstances, have been brought over by, and become prevalent through the medium of, the Christian Church.

Any further consideration of its origin from Christian influences seems to me quite unnecessary, though there are other arguments which might be put. We come, then, to the influence of Aryan culture, which, spreading itself, as its speech indicates, all over the land, is a *vera causa* for such a general cult as well worship. But the evidence, when treated geographically, reveals a state of things which in the end will compel us to conclude that Aryan culture received, rather than generated, well worship in Britain.

Commencing with the Teutonic centers of England, the middle and southeastern counties almost fix the boundary of one form of well worship—a form which has lost all local color, all distinct ritual, and remains only in the dedication of the well or spring to a saint of the Christian Church, in the tradition of its name as a "holy well," or else in the memory of some sort of reverence formerly paid to the waters, which in many cases are nameless. From the coast of Sussex, Kent, Essex, Suffolk, and Norfolk, westward through the land occupied by the South Saxons and Middle English until the territory of west Wales, Wales, and the northern folk is reached, examples are met of wells dedicated to some form of ancient reverence not sufficiently distinct to stamp the nature of the cult.

That Teutonic England should be thus marked off, as we shall presently see by examples, from the rest of Britain and Ireland is a significant fact in favor of the argument that the Teutons did not bring well worship with them, for in the very centers of their settlements and homes its survivals are found in almost the last stages of decay. At one place on the coast, however, an example is found where some details of local ritual are still preserved. This is at Bonchurch, in the Isle of Wight, where, on St. Boniface's Day, the well is decorated with flowers.* We meet with nothing of this kind, however, until we arrive nearer Wales—namely, in Derbyshire, Staffordshire, Worcestershire, and Shropshire. Here is the region of garland-dressing, and the practice has been frequently described. In Worcestershire and Staffordshire the custom is simple. In Derbyshire and Shropshire other practices occur in connection with the well-dressing. For instance, at the holy well at Dale Abbey, in the former county, the devotee goes on Good Friday, between twelve and three o'clock, drinks the water three times, and wishes.† This may be only a survival of monastic practice, but in Shropshire the differentiation is more marked. Garland-dress-

* Tompkins, *Hist. of Isle of Wight*, ii, 121. I can make nothing of the Walsingham wishing-wells except a derivation from monastic ceremonies. See the custom in Brand, ii, 370.

† *Antiquary*, xxi, 97.

ing, though found in the eastern parts of the county, is almost entirely absent from the western, where wishing and healing wells are found.* At Rorrington, a township in the parish of Chirbury, was a holy well at which a wake was celebrated on Ascension Day. The well was adorned with a bower of green boughs, rushes, and flowers, and a May-pole was set up. The people walked round the well, dancing and frolicking as they went. They threw pins into the well to bring good luck and to preserve them from being bewitched, and they also drank some of the water. Cakes were also eaten; they were round flat buns from three to four inches across, sweetened, spiced, and marked with a cross, and they were supposed to bring good luck if kept.†

In this instance garland-dressing is associated with other significant ceremonies, and associated so closely as to suggest that all parts of the ritual are equally ancient. Now, in Shropshire Welsh influence is distinctly felt, and little patches of Welsh population, locally known as Welsheries, exist to this day. I shall leave this part of our examination of Shropshire well worship with the observation that the evidence links on the more elaborate customs there found with the simple customs found in middle and southeastern England, and I shall return to Shropshire later on.

Where the waters of the wells in the district just examined are used for healing powers it is almost invariably the case that the disease to be cured is sore

---

* Burne, *Shropshire Folklore*, p. 414. † Burne, *op. cit.*, p. 434.

eyes; and Miss Burne, who noticed this peculiarity in the Shropshire wells, has made the acute suggestion that a legend in the prose Edda which tells how Odin gave his eye in return for a draught of water from the wisdom-giving well of Mimir, might perhaps account for it.* I think it does; and we have in this parallel between English custom and Scandinavian myth the evidence I am in search of, showing that Teutonic influences on well worship did in fact exist, though they were not powerful enough to keep well worship up as a cult in that part of the country where Teutonic people were most thickly settled.

We next turn to northern England, where the population, Teutonic and Celtic of Aryan folk and the non-Aryan aborigines, were more mixed. The connection between the customs of well worship there and those of the district just examined is established by the existence of garland-dressing in North Lancashire, Westmoreland,† and on the borders.‡ Next we must examine the new features which are significant. At Sefton in Lancashire, it was customary for passers-by to drop into St. Helen's Well a new pin for good luck or to secure the favorable issue of an expressed wish, and by the turning of the pin-point to the north or to any other point of the compass conclusions were drawn as to the fidelity of lovers, date of marriage, and other love matters.# At Brindle is a well dedicated to St. Ellin, where on the

* *Shropshire Folklore*, p. 422.

† *Ibid.*, p. 414.

‡ Henderson, *Folklore*, p. 3.

\# *Antiq.*, xxi, 197.

patron day pins are thrown into the water.* Pin-wells, as they may be called, after the popular name given to them in some places, also existed at Jarrow and Wooler in Northumberland, at Brayton, Minchmore, Kayingham, and Mount Grace in Yorkshire.†

Henderson informs us that "the country girls imagine that the well is in charge of a fairy or spirit who must be propitiated by some offering, and the pin presents itself as the most ready or convenient, besides having a special suitableness as being made of metal."‡ This clearly indicates that the offering in the mind of the peasantry was to be a part of their clothes. At Great Cotes and Winterton in Lincolnshire, Newcastle and Benton in Northumberland, Newton Kyme, Thorp Arch, and Gargrave in Yorkshire, pieces of rag, cloth, or ribbon take the place of the pins, and are tied to bushes adjoining the wells,# while near Newton, at the foot of Roseberry Topping, the shirt or shift of the devotee was thrown into the well, and according to whether it floated or sank so would the sickness leave or be fatal, while as an offering to the saint, a rag of the shirt is torn off and left hanging on the briers thereabouts.‖

It is clear that while there is something in common between the customs attending well worship all over

---

* *Antiq.*, xxi, 197.

† *Antiq.*, xxii, 66, 67; xxiii, 77, 112, 113; xxiv, 27; Henderson, *Folklore*, p. 231.

‡ Henderson, *Folklore*, p. 230.

\# *Antiq.*, xxi, 265; xxii, 30; xxiii, 23, 77; xxiv, 27.

‖ *Gent. Mag. Lib.*, *Superstitions*, pp. 143, 147; Brand, ii, 380.

England, a line of distinction has to be drawn as we proceed farther north. That rag-wells are the ancestors in custom of pin-wells scarcely needs suggestion, but I think we may go on to suggest that the bushes growing around the sacred wells in the north are the ancestors in custom of the bushes brought to decorate the wells in the south, and this is confirmed by the fact that where there are bushes adjoining the wells dressing with garlands does not take place. In the north, too, it must be noted that some wells were under the protection of the fairies or some specially named sprite, as at Brayton, Harpham, Holderness, and Atwick in Yorkshire, and Wooler in Northumberland. The course of well worship in Teutonic England, then, may be traced from the examples of simple reverence in the south and east to examples of garland-dressing and pin-offerings towards the Welsh borders, and to examples, first of garland-dressing and pin-offerings, and finally to the parent form of rag-bush wells toward the northern border. Now rag-bushes have a distinct place in anthropological evidence which must be examined presently. In the mean time we carry on our investigations of well worship in Britain by turning to the forms of the cult in the Celtic-speaking districts.

For this purpose we once more take up the Shropshire evidence, in order to pursue it from its English to its Welsh side. St. Oswald's Well, at Oswestry, is used for wishing and divination. One rite, says Miss Burne, is to go to the well at midnight, take some water up in the hand and drink part of it, at the same time forming a wish in the mind, throw the rest of the water upon a particular stone at the back of the well, and if the votary can succeed in throwing all the water left in his hand upon this stone without touching any other spot, his wish will be fulfilled. Other forms of the ceremony to be adopted for the purpose of gaining the desired end are described,* but they are less distinctive than the one quoted, the point of which is the sprinkling of a special stone with the water from the well. Another element is introduced in the case of the well on the Devil's Causeway between Ruckley and Acton. Here, according to popular belief, the devil and his imps appear in the form of frogs; three frogs are always seen together, and these are the imps, the largest frog, representing the devil, appearing but seldom.† Here for the first time we find the presiding spirit of the well represented in animal form.

Pin-wells in Wales are met with at Rhosgoch in Montgomeryshire,‡ St. Cynhafal's Well in Denbighshire, St. Barruc's Well on Barry Island, near Cardiff, Ffynon Gwynwy spring in Carnarvonshire, and a well near Penrhos.# A new departure in the ritual of well worship, however, occurs in connection with St. Tegla's

---

* Burne, *Shropshire Folklore*, p. 428; other Shropshire examples are given in *Antiq.*, xxii., 253.

† Burne, *op. cit.*, p. 416; *cf.* the Oxfordshire frog-prince story, *Antiq.*, xxii, 68.

‡ *Antiq.*, xxii, 253.

# Wirt Sikes, *British Goblins*, pp. 351, 352, 356.

Well, about half-way between Wrexham and Ruthin. This well is resorted to for the cure of epilepsy. The custom is for the patient to repair to the well after sunset and wash himself in its waters; then, having made an offering by throwing fourpence into the water, to walk round the well three times and thrice repeat the Lord's Prayer. He then offers a cock or, when the patient is a woman, a hen. The bird is carried in a basket first round the well, then round the church. After this the patient enters the church, creeps under the altar, and, making the Bible his pillow and the communion cloth his coverlet, remains there till break of day. In the morning, having made a further offering of sixpence, he leaves the cock and departs. Should the bird die it is supposed that the disease has been transferred to it, and the man or woman consequently cured.* Another and still more remarkable ceremony appertains to the well of St. Ælian, not far from Bettws Abergeley, in Denbighshire. Near the well resided a woman who officiated as a kind of priestess. Any one who wished to inflict a curse upon an enemy resorted to this priestess, and for a trifling sum she registered in a book kept for the purpose the name of the person on whom the curse was wished to fall. A pin was then dropped into the well in the name of the victim, and the curse was complete.†

---

* *Arch. Camb.*, 1st Ser., i, 184; Wirt Sikes, *British Goblins*, p. 329.

† Roberts, *Cambrian Pop. Antiq.*, p. 246; Wirt Sikes, *op. cit.*, p. 355; *Arch. Camb.*, 1st Ser., i, 46.

It is obvious that while the ritual of well worship in Wales is connected by some of its details, notably the offering of pins, with the ritual of English well worship, it contains perfectly distinctive elements, all of which tend toward the interpretation of the cult as of a rude and primitive type. The presiding spirit of the well in animal form in one example equates with the offering to the presiding spirit of a bird in another example, while the curse obtained through the agency of a priestess acting upon the name only of the intended victim presents a new feature. Animal gods and animal offerings to gods mark clear and well-recognized features of primitive ritual, and the efficacy of the name as a tangible part of the person to whom it belongs, besides being represented among general primitive ideas,* is specially connected with the practice of working injury upon an enemy. Thus Ellis mentions an example among the Tshi-speaking people of Africa very nearly allied to the Welsh example. The formula is to take three short sticks, call aloud three times the name of the person to be killed, and while so doing to bind the sticks together and then lay them upon the *suhman* or tutelary deity.†

Now Wales, as Professor Rhys has taught us, forms with Cornwall or West Wales the country of the Brythonic Celts, the second of the two bands of Aryan Celts

* *Cf.* Mr. Clodd's admirable summary of this subject in *Folk-lore Journal*, vii. 135–161.

† Ellis, *Tshi-speaking Peoples*, p. 107.

who invaded and settled down in Britain. We must, then, turn now to examples of well worship in West Wales. Pin-wells and rag-wells are both represented in Cornwall—as, for instance, at Pelynt, St. Austel, and St. Roche, where pins are offered, and at Madron Well, where both pins and rags are offered.* The two fish sacred to St. Neot, and which never decreased or increased in size or number, must be considered as the sacred fish of the well, parallel to the sacred animals we have already seen in Wales; and the idea of the well being under the care of a priestess, which occurred in Denbighshire, appears in the case of Gulval Well, in Fosses Moor. There an old woman was "a sort of guardian to the well," and instructed the devotees in their ceremonial observances. They had to kneel down and lean over the well so as to see their faces in the water, and repeat after their instructor a rhyming incantation, after which, by the bubbling of the water or by its quiescence, the reply of the spirit of the well was interpreted.† At Altarnum Well there is something approaching to human sacrifice. Its special function was the cure of madness, and the afflicted person stood with his back to the pool, and from thence, by a sudden blow in the breast, was tumbled headlong into the water, where a strong fellow took him and tossed him up and down.‡ At Chapel Uny rickety children are

---

* *Antiq.*, xxi. 27, 28, 30; Hunt, *Popular Romances*, p. 295; *Folklore Journal*, ii., 349.

† Hunt, *op. cit.*, p. 291. ‡ *Ibid.*, p. 296.

dipped three times in the well against the sun, and dragged three times round the well in the same direction.*

As a rough summary of the Welsh evidence it may be stated that well worship in the district occupied by the later of the two Celtic invaders of Britain is far ruder and more primitive than in the district occupied by the Teutonic invaders of Britain. Either, then, modern culture has acted more powerfully upon Teutonic England than upon Wales, routing up the pagan rites that existed there, or else Teutonic culture itself acted against the cult of well worship, and so helped to whittle it down to its present insignificance. With regard to the first alternative, there are few scholars acquainted with the long catalogue of significant survivals of Teutonic heathendom in Europe who would be prepared to assert that the Teutons, as a branch of the Aryan race, have been more susceptible to civilization than the Celts. On the second alternative, it may be remarked that so far as Teutonic culture may be considered as Aryan, it would be in all essential matters shared by the Celts, and that hence we should expect Celtic culture to have acted against well worship. But if it be remembered that the Celts were displaced from southeastern Britain by the Teutons and driven into the western lands of Wales and southwest Britain among the otherwise untouched aborigines, the suggestion is at once supplied that the Brythonic Celts were

* Hunt, *Popular Romances*, p. 300.

absorbing in their last home some of the local worships of the conquered aborigines. In South Wales the physical characteristics of this non-Aryan race survive,* and why not, therefore, the remnants of their beliefs, especially those attached to definite local objects? It does not seem possible at this stage to do more than state the hypothesis which the evidence thus suggests, and it remains for us to examine well worship in the districts occupied by the first Aryan invaders, named Goidelic Celts by Professor Rhys, and containing in their language proofs of their ancient incoming into a land of non-Aryans. These districts are situated in Scotland and Ireland.

In Ireland well worship is nearly universal, and the offering of pieces of rag is the invariable accompaniment. Among examples of rag-wells, which show the common basis which the cult has in all parts of the British Isles, may be mentioned Ardclinis, County Antrim; Errigall-Keroge, County Tyrone; Dungiven; St. Bartholomew's Well at Pilltown, County Waterford; and St. Brigid's Well at Cliffony, County Sligo. † At Rathlogan, in Kilkenny, we meet with the cure of sore eyes already noted in Britain, and examples of this are said to be elsewhere frequently met with. ‡

The locality of the Irish wells forms a very inter-

---

* Beddoe, *Races of Britain*, p. 26.

† Mason, *Stat. Acc. of Ireland*. i, 328; iii, 27, 161; *Proc. Roy. Hist. and Arch. Soc. of Ireland*, 4th Ser., v, 370, 382.

‡ *Proc. Roy. Hist. and Arch. Assoc. of Ireland*, 4th Ser., ii, 280.

esting aspect of their history. "Along the old ways and not unfrequently hidden in the fields we discover interesting localities, with traces of ancient boundaries and primitive plantations, their verdant swards and leafy sweetness at once indicating their venerable old age; and where the progress of modern reclamation has not obliterated the landmarks of previous generations the peculiar configuration of those places at once points them out as the scenes of former life and importance, often retaining in the midst of rural silence the name of the "street," the "green," the "common," the "cross," or some other title of equal significance. Here we usually find an insignificant inclosure yet revered as holy ground, here on the appointed day the patron was held, . . . here, too, we find a holy well retaining the name of the ancient patron saint of the locality."* I quote this passage because it proclaims the archaic conditions surrounding the worship of wells—conditions which must be appreciated and understood, if we are to read aright the ethnological evidence to be derived from this section of our subject.

The cult is so general in Ireland that it has not received the attention of Irish antiquaries as it deserves. The presence of animals or fish as guardians or tutelary deities of the wells is a marked feature. The fount of Tober Kieran, near Kells, County Meath, rises in a diminutive rough-sided basin of limestone of natural

* *Proc. Roy. Hist. and Arch. Assoc. of Ireland*, 4th Ser., ii, 266.

formation, and evidently untouched by a tool. In the water are a brace of miraculous trout "which, according to tradition, have occupied their narrow prison from time immemorial. They are said never in the memory of man to have altered in size, and it is said of them that their appearance is ever the same." Within about a mile of Cong, County Galway, is a deep depression in the limestone called "Pigeon Hole," and the sacred rivulet running at the base of the chasm "is believed to contain a pair of enchanted trout," one of which is said to have been captured some time ago by a trooper and cooked, but upon the approach of cold steel "the creature at once changed into a beautiful young woman," and was returned to the stream. The well at Tullaghan, County Sligo, is known both in history and tradition. It is described as one of the wonders of Ireland by Nennius, Giraldus Cambrensis, and O'Flaherty, and it is the subject of a curious legend in the book of "Dinnsenchas"; and a brace of miraculous trout, not always visible to ordinary eyes, are said to have inhabited this pool. At Ballymorereigh, in Dingle, County Kerry, is a sacred well called Tober Monachan, where a salmon and eel appear to devotees who are to be favored by the guardian spirits of this well.*

Thus far the ceremonies of well worship in Ireland present practically the same features, though in a far more intensified form, as those in Wales. The proces-

* *Proc. Roy. Hist. and Arch. Soc. of Ireland*, 4th Ser., v, 366, 367, 370; vii, 656.

sions round the well sunwise are an important and nearly universal part of the ceremony which the Irish evidence introduces into the subject, and the apparently unimportant detail occurring in a Shropshire example noted above, of pouring water over a particular stone, receives significant light from the examples in Ireland. Thus at Dungiven, after hanging their offerings of rags on the bush adjoining the well, the devotees proceed to a large stone in the river Roe immediately below the old church, and, having performed an ablution, they walk round the stone, bowing to it and repeating prayers, and then, after performing a similar ceremony in the church, they finish the rite by a procession and prayer round the upright stone.* But besides restoring the unimportant details of Welsh ritual to an important place in well worship, Irish evidence introduces a wholly new feature. Thus at Tobernacoragh, a sacred well on the island of Innismurray, off the coast of Sligo, during tempestuous weather "it was the custom for the natives to drain the waters of this well into the ocean, as they believed by so doing, and by the offering up of certain prayers, the elemental war might cease and a holy calm follow."† In this case the connection between well worship and the worship of a rain-god is certain, for it may be surmised that if the emptying of the well allayed a storm, some complementary action was practiced at one time or other in order to produce

* Mason, *Stat. Acc. of Ireland*, i, 328.

† *Proc. Roy. Hist. and Arch. Soc. of Ireland*, 4th Ser., vii, 300.

rain, and in districts more subject to a want of rain than this Atlantic island that ceremony would be accentuated at the expense of the storm-allaying ceremony at Innismurray.

Finally we pass into Scotland, where also the Goidelic Celts settled. I will first briefly enumerate some instances to show the identity of customs connected with well worship in Scotland with those in the districts we have already examined. This will confirm the evidence, which seems to be pretty well established, that the foundation of well worship in all parts of the British Isles is the same—the rites and ceremonies are substantially part and parcel of a common cult; they differ in the degree in which they have survived in various places, but the forms of the survival do not differ in kind, because they are derived from a common origin.

About fifty years after the Reformation it was noted that the wells of Scotland "were all tapestried about with old rags."* The best examples lasting to within modern times are to be found in the islands round the coast, and in the northern shires, particularly in Banff, Aberdeen, Perth, Ross, and Caithness. At Kilmuir, in the Isle of Skye, at Loch Shiant, or Siant, there was "a shelf made in the wall of a contiguous inclosure" for placing thereon "the offerings of small rags, pins, and colored threads to the divinity of the place."† At St.

* *The Book of Bon Accord*, p. 268.

† Sinclair's *Stat. Acc. of Scotland*, ii, 557; *New Stat. Acc.* xiv, 245; Martin, *Western Isles*, p. 140.

Mourie's Well, on Malruba Isle, a rag was left on the bushes, nails stuck into an oak tree, or sometimes a copper coin driven in.* At Toubirmore Well, in Gigha Isle, devotees were accustomed to leave "a piece of money, a needle, pin, or one of the prettiest variegated stones they could find," and at Tonbir Well, in Jura, they left "an offering of some small token, such as a pin, needle, farthing, or the like." † In Banffshire, at Montblairie, "many still alive remember to have seen the impending boughs adorned with rags of linen and woolen garments, and the well enriched with farthings and bodles, the offerings of those who came from afar to the fountain." ‡ At Keith the well is near a stone circle, and some offering was always left by the devotees.# In Aberdeenshire, at Fraserburgh, "the superstitious practice of leaving some small trifle" existed. ‖ In Perthshire, at St. Fillan's Well, Comrie, the patients leave behind "some rags of linen or woolen cloth." ^ In Caithness, at Dunnet, they throw a piece of money in the water, and at Wick they leave a piece of bread and cheese and a silver coin, which they alleged disappeared in some mysterious way. ◊ In Ross and Cromarty, at Alness, "pieces of colored cloth were left as offerings"; at Cragnick an offering of a rag was sus-

---

* Gordon Cumming, *In the Hebrides*, pp. 190, 191.

† Martin's *Tour*, pp. 230, 242.

‡ Robertson, *Antiquities of Aberdeen and Banff*, ii, 310.

\# Sinclair's *Stat. Acc of Scot.*, v, 430.

‖ *Ibid.*, vi, 9. ^ *Ibid.*, xi, 181.

◊ *New Stat. Acc.*, xv, 38, 161.

pended from a bramble bush overhanging the well; at Fodderty the devotees "always left on a neighboring bush or tree a bit of colored cloth or thread as a relic; and at Kiltearn shreds of clothing were hung on the surrounding trees.* In Sutherlandshire, at Farr and at Loth, a coin was thrown into the well.† In Dumfriesshire, at Penpont, a part of the dress was left as an offering, and many pieces have been seen "floating on the lake or scattered round the banks."‡ In Kirkcud-brightshire, at Buittle, "either money or clothes" was left,# and in Renfrewshire, at Houston, "pieces of cloth were left as a present or offering to the saint on the bushes."‖

These examples give a fair idea of what may be found on this subject by searching among the older topographical accounts. It is scarcely necessary to pursue these details with greater minuteness, and it may be stated as a general rule that "at all these fountains the invalid used the same ceremonies, approaching them sunwise,"△ or "deisil," as it was called. Nowhere is this particular so prominent as in Scotland, and it should be borne in mind in connection with the other ceremonies performed at the wells.

There are now some more special details to note. The cure of madness by severe physical measures, such as we have noted in Ireland, is represented in Scotland

---

* *New Stat. Acc.*, xiv, 246, 344, 382; Sinclair, i, 284.

† *New Stat. Acc.*, xv, 72, 191.

‡ *Ibid.*, iv, 506.

\# *Ibid.*, iv, 203.

‖ Sinclair's *Stat. Acc.*, i, 316.

△ Forbes Leslie, *Early Races of Scotland*, i, p. 156.

in Lochmaree Island, where, after drinking from the well, the patients were towed round the island;* at Strathfillan, near Logierait, where the patient bathed after sunset and before sunrise the next morning, and was then laid on his back bound to a stone in the ruined chapel of St. Fillan, and if next morning he was found loose the cure was deemed perfect.† An important feature of this ceremony is the time—during the absence of the sun. At Farr, in Sutherlandshire, the patient, after undergoing his plunge, drinking of the water, and making his offering, "must be away from the banks so as to be fairly out of sight of the water before the sun rises, else no cure is effected."‡ On the other hand, to bathe in the well of St. Medan, at Kirkmaiden in Wigtonshire, as the sun rose on the first Sunday in May was considered an infallible cure for almost any disease.# At Cragnick Well, at Avoch, in Ross, bathing took place under the same conditions as to time and date, but it was also necessary to spill a portion of the water upon the ground three times.‖ At Muthill, in Perthshire, the time for drinking the waters was before the sun rises or immediately after it sets, coupled with the condition that it was to be drunk out of a "quick cow's horn" (a horn taken from a live cow); "which indispensable horn was in the keeping of an old woman who lived near the well."^

---

* *New Stat., Acc. of Scot*, xiv, 92. † *New Stat. Acc.*, x, 1088.
‡ *Ibid.*, xv, 72. # *Ibid.*, iv, 208. ‖ *Ibid.*, xiv, 382.
^ *Ibid.*, x, 313.

This latter custom reintroduces the idea of a priestess of the well, which we have seen first appears in Wales. Perhaps the leaving of a piece of silver or gold in the water "for the officiating priest" at Loth, in Sutherlandshire,* may be a survival of the same idea, but I think the survival is undoubted in those cases where the patient does not attend at the well himself, but employs a substitute. It is noticeable that this substitute has to go through a most careful ceremonial. Thus at Penpont, in Dumfriesshire, the emissary of the patient, when he reached the well, "had to draw water in a vessel which was on no account to touch the ground, to turn himself round with the sun, to throw his offering to the spirit over his left shoulder and to carry the water without ever looking back to the sick person. All this was to be done in absolute silence, and he was to salute no one by the way." † The elements of magic ritual preserved here are very obvious, and it is to be remarked that silence is a condition imposed upon the devotees at many wells in Ireland and also in England.

In the Isle of Lewis occurs a remarkable variant. "St. Andrew's Well, in the village Shadar," says Martin, "is by the vulgar natives made a test to know if a sick person will die of the distemper he labors under. They send one with a wooden dish to bring some of the water to the patient, and if the dish, which is then laid softly upon the surface of the water, turn round sunways they conclude that the patient will recover of

* *New Stat. Acc.*, xv, 191. † *Stat. Acc. of Scot.*, iv, 506.

that distemper, but if otherwise, that he will die."* I am inclined to connect this with the vessel or caldron so frequently occurring in Celtic tradition, and which Mr. Nutt has marked as "a part of the gear of the oldest Celtic divinities,"† perhaps of divinities older than the Celts.

The connection between well worship and the cult of the rain-god appeared in the example at Innismurray Island, off the coast of Sligo. It also is a feature of the Scottish evidence. The well of Tarbat, in the island of Gigha, "is famous for having the command of the wind. Six feet above where the water gushes out there is a heap of stones, which forms a cover to the sacred fount. When a person wished for a fair wind this part was opened with great solemnity, the stones carefully removed, and the well cleaned with a wooden dish or clam-shell. This being done, the water was several times thrown in the direction from which the wished-for wind was to blow, and this action was accompanied by a certain form of words, which the person repeated every time he threw the water. When the ceremony was over the well was again carefully shut up to prevent fatal consequences, it being firmly believed that were the place left open it would occasion a storm which would overwhelm the whole island."‡ When to

---

* Martin, *Western Islands*, p. 7.

† *Studies in the Legend of the Holy Grail*, p. 185, and compare the magic cup in the Karen River legend.—*Journ. As. Soc. Bengal*, xxxiv, (2) 219.

‡ Sinclair's *Stat., Acc.*, viii, 52; Martin, *Western Islands*, p. 230.

these striking details of magical ritual is added the fact that there were two old woman "who are said to have the secret," and through whom the ceremonial is to be accomplished, one can not but recognize the parallel to those priestesses of Sena and their rites with which classical authorities have acquainted us. One little detail is recorded by Martin which is not given in the otherwise fuller account just quoted—namely, that the well must always be "opened by a diroch, i. e., an inmate, else they think it would not exert its virtues," and this emphasis on the necessity of action being taken by a native as opposed to a foreigner or strangor is again recorded of a well rite in the island of Egg, where, "if a stranger lie at this well in the night-time it will procure a deformity in some part of his body, but has no such effect on a native." *

Finally, as to the guardian spirit of the Scottish wells. At Kilbride, in Skye, was a well with "one trout only in it; the natives are very tender of it, and though they often chance to catch it in their wooden pails, they are very careful to preserve it from being destroyed." † In the well at Kilmore, in Lorn, were two fish, black in color, never augmenting in size or number nor exhibiting any alteration of color, and the inhabitants of the place "doe call the saide fishes Easg Siant, that is to say, holie fishes." ‡ This supplies an exact counterpart of the Irish beliefs. Other examples of a still

* Martin, *op cit.*, p. 277. † *Ibid.*, p. 141.

‡ Dalyell, *Darker Superstitions*, p. 412.

more interesting nature occur in Scotland, however. If, says Dalyell, a certain worm in a medicinal spring on the top of the hill in the parish of Strathdon were found alive it augured the recovery of a patient, and in a well of Ardnacloich, in Appin, the patient "if he bee to dye shall find a dead worme therein, or a quick one, if health bee to follow."* These, there can be little doubt, are the former deities of the spring thus reduced in status. But the most remarkable example occurs at a well near the church of Kirkmichael, in Banffshire. The guardian of the well assumed the semblance of a fly, who was always present, and whose every movement was regarded by the votaries at the shrine with silent awe, and as he appeared cheerful or dejected the anxious votaries drew their presages. This guardian fly of the well of St. Michael was believed to be exempt from the laws of mortality. "To the eye of ignorance," says the local account, "he might sometimes appear dead, but it was only a transmigration into a similiar form, which made little alteration to the real identity."† It seems impossible to mistake this as an almost perfect example where the guardian deity of the sacred spring is represented in animal form. More perfect than any other example to be met with in Britain and its isles is this singular description of the traditional peasant belief; it lifts the whole evidence as to the identification of wells in Britain as the shrine of ancient local deities

* Dalyell, *op. cit.*. 506, 507.

† Sinclair's *Stat. Acc. of Scot.*, xii, 465.

into close parallel with savage ideas and thought. The divine life of the waters, as Professor Robertson Smith says, resides in the sacred fish that inhabits them, and he gives numerous examples analogous to the Scottish and Irish. But whether represented by fish, or frog, or worm, or fly, "in all their various forms, the point of the legends is that the sacred source is either inhabited by a demoniac being or imbued with demoniac life." *

This is the highest point to be reached in the survey of well worship in Britain. The animal god is clearly an element of the primitive life of the worshipers at these wells, and it is here that research into origins must commence. From the small beginnings, where the survival of some ancient cult is represented by the simple idea of reverence for certain wells mostly dedicated to a Christian saint, through stages where a ceremonial is faintly traced in the well-dressing with garlands decked with flowers and ribbons; where shrubs and trees growing near the well are the recipients of offerings by devotees to the spirit of the well; where disease and sickness of all kinds are ministered to; where aid is sought against enemies; where the gift of rain is obtained; where the spirit appears in general forms as fairies and in specific form as animal or fish, and finally, it may be, in anthropomorphic form as Christian saint; where priestesses attended the well to preside over the ceremonies; with the several variants overlapping at

* *Religion of the Semites*, p. 161.

every stage, and thus keeping the whole group of superstition and custom in touch one section with another; with the curious local details cropping up to illumine the atmosphere of pagan worship which is so evidently the basis of reverence for wells—there is every reason to identify this cult as the most widespread and the most lasting in connection with local natural objects. The deification of rivers, of mountain tops, of crags and weird places obtains here and there only; the deification of the waters of the well occurs all over the land. And we are met with a very important fact of classification—that it is in the Celtic-speaking districts of our land where the rudest and most uncivilized ceremonial is extant, and, further, that it is in the country of the Goidelic, or earliest branch of the Celts, where this finds its most pronounced types.

To show how this may be translated into terms of ethnology it will be best to reduce it into something like a formula. It must be remembered that we are dealing with survivals of an ancient cult, and the point is to ascertain where the survivals are the most perfect—less touched, that is, by the incoming civilizations which have swept over them. This formula might perhaps be arranged as shown by the table on the next page.

From this it is clear that we may take the acts of simple reverence, garland-dressing, and dedication to a Christian saint as the late expression in popular tradition of the earlier and more primitive acts tabulated above. Taking the more primitive elements as our basis, the lowest point is obtained from English ground, which only rises into the primitive stage in the northern counties, where rag-bushes are found. On Welsh ground the highest point of primitive culture is the tradition of an animal guardian spirit. On Irish ground the highest point is the identification of the well deity with the rain-god, while on Scottish ground the highest points recognizable elsewhere are accentuated in degree.

| | FORM OF WORSHIP. | | | | | OFFERINGS. | | | DEITY OR SPIRIT. | | | |
|---|---|---|---|---|---|---|---|---|---|---|---|---|
| | Simple reverence. | Cure of disease. | Wishing and divination. | Rain-producing. | Sun-worship influences. | Garland-dressing. | Pins. | Rag-bushes. | Saint. | Fairy. | Animal genius. | Human priest or priestess. |
| England: | | | | | | | | | | | | |
| Eastern and South-eastern | + | | | | | | | | + | | | |
| Isle of Wight | + | | | | | + | | | + | | | |
| Western (middle) | + | | | | | + | | | + | | | |
| Western | | + | + | | | + | + | | + | | | |
| Northern (*a*) | | + | + | | | + | + | | + | | | |
| " (*b*) | | + | + | | | | + | + | | + | | |
| Wales | | + | + | | + | | + | | | | + | + |
| Cornwall | | + | + | | + | | | | | | + | + |
| Ireland | | + | + | + | + | | | + | | | + | |
| Scotland | | + | + | + | + | | | + | | | + | + |

Now, I have proved above that the three forms in which offerings to the well deities are made are but variants of one primitive form—namely, the offerings of rags or parts of clothing upon bushes sacred to the well. This species of offering has been investigated with regard to its geographical distribution by Mr. M. J. Walhouse, and it is certain that it occupies a much wider area than that inhabited by Aryan peoples.* Thus, to quote a summary given by General Pitt-Rivers: "Burton says it extends throughout northern Africa from west to east; Mungo Park mentions it in western Africa; Sir Samuel Baker speaks of it on the confines of Abyssinia, and says that the people who practiced it were unable to assign a reason for doing so; Burton also found the same custom in Arabia during his pilgrimage to Mecca; in Persia Sir William Ouseley saw a tree close to a large monolith covered with these rags, and he describes it as a practice appertaining to a religion long since proscribed in that country; in the Dekkan and Ceylon Colonel Leslie says that the trees in the neighborhood of wells may be seen covered with similar scraps of cotton; Dr. A. Campbell speaks of it as being practiced by the Limboos near Darjeeling in the Himalaya, where it is associated, as in Ireland, with large heaps of stones; and Huc in his travels mentions it among the Tartars." † Here not only do we get evidence of the cult in an Aryan country like Persia being proscribed, but, as General Pitt-Rivers observes, "it is impossible to believe that so singular a custom as this, invariably associated with cairns, megalithic monuments, holy wells, or some such early pagan institutions, could have arisen independently in all these countries." That the area over which it is found is coterminous with the area of the megalithic monuments, that these monuments take us back to pre-Aryan people

* *Journ. Anthrop. Inst.*, ix, 97–106.

† *Journ. Ethnol. Soc.*, N. S., i, 64.

and suggest the spread of this people over the area covered by their remains, are arguments in favor of a megalithic date for well worship and rag offerings.

That I am concerned only with the element of ethnology in this cult compels me to pass over the very important conclusions which an analysis of the rites of well worship suggests in connection with the primitive agricultural life of the pre-Aryan people of these islands, and I conclude what there is to say about well worship by a reference to a chronological fact of some interest and importance.

Its highest form of rude savagery within the area which we have examined so minutely is found in the country of the old Picts of Scotland, who are identified as non-Aryans by Professor Rhys. And this was the country where St. Columba found a "fountain famous among this heathen people [and] worshiped as a god," and where in its waters he vanquished and confounded "the Druids" and "then blessed the fountain, and from that day the demons separated from the water." * In this non-Aryan country, as in ancient and perhaps pre-Semitic Arabia, "the fountain is treated as a living thing, those properties of its waters which we call natural are regarded as manifestations of a divine life, and the source itself is honored as a divine being, I had almost said a divine animal." † This pregnant

---

* Reeve's edition of *Adamnan's Life of St. Columba*, lib. ii, cap. xi.

† Robertson Smith, *Religion of the Semites*, p. 168.

summary of well worship in Arabia may without the alteration of a single word be adopted as the summary of well worship in Britain and its isles, and it confirms the conclusion that it is a non-Aryan cult attached to the most important of natural objects, which existed before Celt or Teuton spread over the land, and which retained, as in Pictland we have definite evidence, all the old faiths, whatsoever people might come and settle down around them.

The power of localization in primitive belief is shown by these examples to have been a very significant and lasting power. Research could be extended into other branches of the subject—to mountain worship, tree worship, rock worship; but extension would do no more than confirm what I hope is now clear—that some of the great objects of nature common to all localities, conspicuous to all people living in the localities, generated certain beliefs which remain permanently fixed upon the object, and thus afford lasting evidence of the continuity of early faiths which do not cease when newer faiths come into contact with them.

# CHAPTER V.

## THE ETHNIC GENEALOGY OF FOLKLORE.

THE analogies which exist between savage custom and European folklore suggested the first stage of the argument for the existence of ethnic elements in folklore. What is this folklore, which can be traced to nothing, outside of folklore, in the habitual beliefs and customs of civilized countries, and which is parallel only to the habitual beliefs and customs of savages? A key to the answer was supplied when it was pointed out that there is an equation which consists, on the one side, of Indian religious rites, in which Aryan and non-Aryan races take their respective parts, and, on the other side, of custom in survival among European peasantry. From this it was argued that the appearance of the factor of race on one side of the equation made it necessary that it should also be inserted on the other side, and it was therefore urged that the items of folklore thus ear-marked should be separated off into groups of non-Aryan and Aryan origins.

It follows from this, then, that relics of *different* races are to be found in the folklore of countries whose chief characteristics have up to the present been identified by scholars as belonging to *one* race. So important a conclusion necessitates some further inquiry into those items of folklore on the European side of the equation which are thus allocated to different race origins, and it may be urged that they should contain some quality which of itself, now that we have the key, will help to identify them as of non-Aryan or Aryan origin. We must not, in short, rely upon the comparative method for everything. Aryan belief and custom, though doubtless not easily distinguishable in some cases from non-Aryan belief and custom, is in other cases definitely and distinctly marked off from it both in theory and practice. In folklore, therefore, this difference would also appear if the hypothesis as to origin is true. There must at least exist some beliefs and some usages which are inconsistent with the corresponding Aryan beliefs and usages—an inconsistency which in the last stages of survival does not perhaps present a very important consideration to the peasantry among whom the folklore obtains, but which, if traced back to the originals, may be shown to have been an important factor in the development of primitive Aryan thought and custom.

Hence, in attempting to trace out the originals of modern folklore, it is clear that its inconsistencies must be carefully observed. For the purpose of the problem now under discussion we must note these inconsistencies, in order to see if they may be identified with two distinct lines of primitive custom and belief. On the one hand there would be the line of parallel to modern savagery, where the folklore, that is, is at the same level of development in human culture as the savage custom or belief; on the other hand, there would be the line of parallel to a much higher culture than savagery. If these two inconsistent lines of development are both represented in folklore, though in spirit antagonistic to each other, the point is gained that in folklore is discoverable at least two separate lines of descent. They must have been produced by the presence within the country where they now survive of different races living together in the relationship of conquered and conquerors; they must have been subsequently handed on by generation after generation of the same races; they must finally have been preserved by the peasantry long after distinction of race in Europe had ceased to exist, as mere observance of custom, because, as such, they were part and parcel of their stock of life-action, not pushed out of existence by anything higher in religion or culture, but retaining their old place year after year, decade after decade, simply because their dislodgment, without adequate replacement from other sources, would have created a vacuum as foreign to nature in man as to nature in the world surrounding man.

We have thus two distinct lines of parallel to trace out—a parallel with savagery and a parallel with a higher culture. The work before us is not one that can be accomplished off-hand. Folklore has a genealogy, so to speak, where the links are represented by the various changes which the condition of survival inevitably brings about. I have said that there is no development in folklore. All chances of development had been crushed out when the original elements of what is now classed as folklore were pushed back from the condition of tribal or national custom and belief to that of tolerated peasant superstition. But this does not mean that no change of any sort has taken place. The changes of decay, degradation, and misapplication have taken the place of change by development.

The marked features of these changes are capable of some classification, and I shall term them symbolism, substitution, and amalgamation. A practice originally in one particular form assumes another form, but still symbolical of the original; or it is transferred to another object or set of objects; or it becomes joined on to other practices and beliefs, and produces in this way a new amalgamation. All these processes indicate the change of decay incidental to survivals, not the change of development, and in tracing out the genealogy of folklore it is the changes of decay which mark the steps of the descent. When children are made to jump through the midsummer fires for luck, human sacrifice has in folklore become symbolized; when the blood of the cock is sprinkled, as in France, over the stones of a new building, the animal object of the sacrifice has been substituted for the human object; when the wise man of the Yorkshire villages has assumed the character of part wizard or witch, part sorcerer, magician, or enchanter, and part conjurer, there has been an amalgamation of the characters and credentials of three or four entities in pagan priesthood. And so through all these changes we must endeavor to carefully work back step by step to the original form. That form as restored will represent the true survival enshrined in folklore, and according to its equation with savage, or with an ascertained development from savage originals, will it be possible to decide to what early race it is to be attributed—the highly organized Aryan, capable of a culture equal to his language, or the ruder and more savage predecessors of the Aryan people.

I will now give some examples of the ethnic genealogy of folklore on the lines just traced out. They are examples chosen not for the special object of endeavoring to prove a point, but as evidence of what a careful examination of folklore in detail and in relation to its several component elements might produce if it were systematically and carefully pursued in this manner. The study is laborious, but the results are correspondingly valuable, particularly when it appears that from no other branch of knowledge can we hope to obtain information as to what our ancestors thought and believed.

1. As an act of sorcery the mold from the churchyard, known as the "meels," was in northeastern Scotland used for throwing into the mill-race in order to stop the mill-wheel.* That the mold is not used because it is a consecrated element of the churchyard is suggested by the harmful result expected, and its con-

* Gregor, *Folklore*, p. 216.

nection with the dead is the only alternative cause for its use; so that our examination of this superstitious practice points to some as yet unexplained use of products closely connected with the dead. The importance of this conclusion is shown by an Irish usage—people taking the clay or mold from the graves of priests and boiling it with milk as a decoction for the cure of disease.* Again, in Shetland, a stitch in the side was cured by applying to the part some mold dug from a grave and heated, it being an essential of the ceremony that it must be taken from and returned to the grave before sunset.† In these cases the grave mold is used as food, and it is this circumstance more than the supposed cures effected by it which must be taken as the lowest point in the genealogy of this item of folklore.

The next link in the genealogy shows that the use of grave-mold is only a substitution for the use of the corpse itself. The Irish have a superstition that to dip the left hand of a corpse in the milk-pail has the effect of making the milk produce considerably more cream and of a richer and better kind.‡ A new element presented by the analysis of this form of the custom is that the result is not connected with the cure of disease but

* Wilde's *Beauties of the Boyne*, p. 45; Croker, *Researches in the South of Ireland*, p. 170; *cf. Rev. Celt.*, v, 358. The dew collected from the grave of the last man buried in the churchyard as an application for the cure of goitre may perhaps be a remnant of this class of belief. It occurs at Launceston.—Dyer, *English Folklore*, p. 150.

† Rogers, *Social Life in Scotland*, iii, 226.

‡ Croker, *op. cit.*, p. 234.

with the increase of dairy produce. The limitation to a particular part of the dead body, the left hand, disappears in a custom once obtaining at Oran, in Roscommon. There a child was disinterred and its arms cut off, to be employed in the performance of certain mystic rites, the nature of which, unfortunately, are not stated by my authority.* Scottish witches are credited with opening graves for the purpose of taking out joints of the fingers and toes of dead bodies, with some of the winding sheet, in order to prepare a powder for their magical purposes.† In Lincolnshire a small portion of the human skull was taken from the graveyard and grated, to be used in a mixture and eaten for the cure of fits.‡ For the cure of epilepsy, near Kirkwall, a similar practice was resorted to, while in Caithness and the western isles the patient was made to drink from a suicide's skull.#

Fresh light is thrown upon the nature of the magical practices alluded to in these examples by the evidence afforded by Scottish trials for witchcraft. From the trial of John Brugh, November 24, 1643, it appears that he went to the churchyard of Glendovan on three several occasions, and each time took up a corpse. "The flesch of the quhilk corps was put aboue the byre and stable-dure headis" of certain individuals to de-

* Wilde, *Irish Popular Superstitions*, p. 28.

† Brand, *Pop. Antiq.*, iii, 10.

‡ Dyer, *English Folklore*, p. 147.

\# Rogers, *Social Life in Scotland*, iii, 225.

stroy their cattle.* This practice, when subjected to analysis, becomes divided into two heads:

1. The distribution of human flesh among owners of cattle.

2. The object of such distribution to do harm to these cattle-owners.

We have thus arrived, step by step, at the bodies of the dead being used for some undetermined purposes. Another group of such practices surviving in folklore represents by symbolization a still further step in the genealogy. A note by Bishop White Kennet speaks of a "custom which lately obtained at Amersden, in the county of Oxford, where at the burial of every corps one cake and one flaggon of ale just after the interment were brought to the minister in the church porch."† This, in the opinion of the writer, seems "a remainder" of the custom of sin-eating, and it is probable he is right. The sin-eating custom is thus given by Aubrey: "In the county of Hereford was an old custome at funeralls to have poor people who were to take upon them all the sinnes of the party deceased. The manner was, that when the corps was brought out of the house and layd on the biere, a loafe of bread was brought out and delivered to the sinne-eater over the corps, as also a mazar bowle of maple (gossips bowle) full of beer, which he was to drinke up, and sixpence in money, in consideration whereof he tooke upon him (*ipso facto*)

* Dalyell, *Darker Superstitions of Scotland*, p. 379.

† Aubrey's *Remaines of Gentilisme*, p. 24.

all the sinnes of the defunct, and freed him or her from walking after they were dead." * Aubrey specifically mentions Hereford, Ross, Dynder ("*volens nolens* the parson of ye Parish"), and "in other places in this countie," as also in Breconshire, at Llangors, "where Mr. Gwin, the minister, about 1640, could no hinder ye performing of this ancient custome," and in North Wales, where, instead of a "bowle of beere they have a bowle of milke."

This account is circumstantial enough. Bagford, in his well-known letter to Hearne (1715), mentions the same custom as obtaining in Shropshire, "in those villages adjoyning to Wales." His account is: "When a person dyed there was notice given to an old sire (for so they called him), who presently repaired to the place where the deceased lay and stood before the door of the house, when some of the family came out and furnished him with a cricket, on which he sat down facing the door. Then they gave him a groat which he put in his pocket; a crust of bread which he ate; and a full bowle off ale which he drank off at a draught. After this he got up from the cricket and pronounced with a composed gesture the ease and rest of the soul departed, for which he would pawn his own soul." † There seems some evidence of this custom being in vogue at Llandebie, near Swansea, until about 1850,‡ where the

* Aubrey's *Remaines of Gentilisme*, pp. 35, 36.

† Leland's *Collectanea*, i, lxxvi.

‡ *Archæologia Cambrensis*, iii, 330; *Journ. Anthrop., Inst.*, v,

ceremony was not unlike that described as having been practiced in the west of Scotland. "There were persons," says Mr. Napier, "calling themselves sin-eaters, who when a person died were sent for to come and eat the sins of the deceased. When they came their *modus operandi* was to place a plate of salt and a plate of bread on the breast of the corpse and repeat a series of incantations, after which they ate the contents of the plates and so relieved the dead person of such sins as would have kept him hovering around his relations, haunting them with his imperfectly purified spirit, to their great annoyance and without satisfaction to himself."* The Welsh custom, as described by Mr. Moggridge, adds one important detail not noted with reference to the other customs—namely, that after the cere-

423; Wirt Sikes, *British Goblins*, pp. 326, 327. The Welsh practice of the relatives of the deceased distributing bread and cheese to the poor *over the coffin* seems to me to confirm the evidence for the Welsh sin-eater. One of Elfric's canons says, *inter alia*, "Do not eat and drink over the body in the heathenish manner."—Wilkins, *Concilia*, i, 255.

* Napier, *Folklore of the West of Scotland*, p. 60. I am not quite satisfied with this example. Mr. Napier evidently is not minutely describing an actual observance, and in his book he frequently refers to customs elsewhere. In this instance he does not appear to be alluding to any other than Scottish customs, and it is to be noted that his details differ from Aubrey's and Bagford's, nor can I trace any authority for his details except his own observation, unless it be from Mr. Moggridge's account in *Arch. Cambrensis*, which, however, it does not follow exactly. He is so reliable in respect of all his own notes that I should not doubt this if it were not for the certain amount of vagueness about this passage.

mony the sin-eater "vanished as quickly as possible from the general gaze."

The chief points in these remarkable customs are:

(1) The action of passing the food over the corpse, as if thereby to signify some connection with the corpse.

(2) The immediate disappearance of the sin-eater; and

(3) The object of the ceremony to prevent the spirit of the deceased from annoying the living.

In these customs clearly something is symbolized by the supposed eating up of the sins of the deceased.* As Mr. Frazer has observed in reference to these practices, "the idea of sin is not primitive." † I do not think with Mr. Frazer that the older idea was that death was carried away from the survivors. Something much less subtle than this must have originated all these practices, or they could not have been kept up in so materialistic a form. Folklore tends to become less material as it decays; it goes off into almost shadowy conceptions, not into practices which of themselves are horrid and revolting. These practices, then, must be the indicator which will help us to translate the symbolism of folklore into the usage of primitive life. The various forms

---

* I must acknowledge my indebtedness to Mr. Hartland for the use I make of the custom of sin-eating. He was good enough to draw my attention to a study of the subject he was preparing, and which since the above passage was written he has read before the Folklore Society.

† Frazer, *Golden Bough*, ii. 152, *note*; Miss Burne also seems to suggest this idea (*Shropshire Folklore*, p. 202).

of the survival seem to indicate that we have here a group of customs and beliefs relating to some unknown cult of the dead—a cult which, when it was relegated to the position of a survival by some foreign force which arrested development and only brought decay and change, showed no tendency toward any high conception of future bliss for the deceased in spirit-land; a cult which was savage in conception, savage in the methods of carrying out the central idea which promoted it, savage, too, in the results which must have flowed from it and affected the minds and associations of its actors.

What is the savage idea connected with the dead which underlies these gloomy and disgusting practices preserved in folklore? Let me recall a passage in Strabo relating to the practices of early British savages. The inhabitants of Ireland were cannibals, but they also "deemed it honorable to eat the bodies of their deceased parents." * Now, the eating of dead kindred is a rite practiced by savages in many parts of the world, and it is founded primarily on the fear which savage man had for the spirits of the dead.

The conception of fear in connection with the dead is still retained in folklore. Miss Burne, with great reason, attributes the popular objection to carrying a corpse along a private road to the dread lest the dead should come back by the road the corpse traveled.† In Scotland the same dread is expressed by the curious

* Strabo, lib. iv, cap. v, sect. 4.

† *Shropshire Folklore*, p. 303.

practice of turning upside down all the chairs in the room from which the corpse has just been taken;* in England by the practice of unhinging the gate and placing it across the entrance, and of carrying the corpse to the grave by a roundabout way.† There is also the practice in Scotland of keeping up a dance all night after a funeral,‡ which by the analogous practice among the Nagas of India must be attributed to the desire to get rid of the spirit of the deceased.# The Caithness Scots, too, share with some South African tribes a deep-rooted reluctance to speak of a man as dead.‖ The point of these practices is that the returning ghosts are not friendly to their earthly kindred, do not represent the idea of friendly ancestral spirits who, in their newly-assumed character of spirits, will help their kindred on earth to get through the troubles of life. The mere fear of ghosts, which is the outcome of modern superstition, does not account for these practices, because it does not cover the wide area occupied by them in savage life which Mr. Frazer has so skillfully traveled over. In this connection, too, I would mention that, associated with the outcast and the criminal, the same idea of fear

* *Folklore Record*, ii, 214.

† Frazer, in *Journ. Anthrop. Inst.*, xv, 72.

‡ Napier, *Folklore of West of Scotland*, p. 66; *Folklore Journal*, iii, 281; Pococke's *Tour through Scotland*, 1760, p. 88.

# Owen's *Notes on the Naga Tribes*, p. 23.

‖ *Journ. Anthrop. Inst.*, xx, 121; Lubbock, *Prehistoric Times*, p. 471: it is also an Australian belief.—*Trans. Ethnol. Soc.*, i, 299, iii, 40.

for the ghosts of the dead is perfectly obvious, which introduces the further suggestion that in this case we have evidence of a certain degraded class of the modern population becoming identified in the peasant mind—in the minds of those, that is, who have kept alive the oldest instincts of prehistoric times—with the ideas and practices which once belonged to a fallen and degraded race existing in their midst. For my present purpose I will quote from Mr. Atkinson the following passage: "There is no doubt that the self-murderer or the doer of some atrocious deed of violence, murder, or lust was buried by some lonely roadside, in a road-crossing, or by the wild woodside, and that the oak, or oftener thorn stake, was driven through his breast. These characters could not rest in their graves. They had to wander about the scenes of their crimes or the places where their unhallowed carcasses were deposited, unless they were prevented, and as they wanted the semblance, the *simulacrum*, the shadow substance of their bodies, for that purpose, the body was made secure by pinning it to the bottom of the grave by aid of the driven stake. And there were other means adopted with the same end in view. The head was severed from the body and laid between the legs or placed under the arm—between the side and the arm, that is—or the feet and legs were bound together with a strong rope; or the corpse might be cut up into some hollow vessel capable of containing the pieces, and carried away quite beyond the precincts of the village and deposited in some bog or morass."* These ghastly ceremonies throw much light on the old folk-belief as to the dead. What is now confined to the suicide or criminal in parts of England is identical with ceremonies performed by savage tribes for all their dead, and it is impossible to put on one side the suggestion that we have in this partial survival relics of a conception of the dead which once belonged to an ethnic division of the people, and not to a caste created by the laws of crime.

I am anxious in this first attempt at definitely tracing out the genealogy of a particular element in folklore to show clearly that the process is a justifiable one. It will not be possible in all instances to do this, partly on account of space and partly on account of the singular diversity of the evidence. But in this instance the attempt may perhaps be made, and I will first proceed to set down, in the usual manner of a genealogy, the various stages already noted in this case, and I will then set down the parallel genealogy supplied from savagery.

---

* Atkinson, *Forty Years in a Moorland Parish*, pp. 217, 218. The modern reason for these doings is the idea of "ignominy, abhorrence, execration, or what not."

† Ancient Peruvians (Dormer, *Origin of Primitive Superstitions*, p. 151; Hakluyt, *Rites of the Incas*, p. 94); Battahs of Sumatra (Featherman, *Soc. Hist.*, 2d div., 336; *Journ. Ind. Arch.*, ii, 241; Marsden, *Sumatra*, p. 390); Philippine Islanders (Featherman. *op. cit.*, p. 496); Gonds and Kookies of India (Rowney, *Wild Tribes of India*, p. 7; *Journ. As. Soc. Bengal*, xvi, 14); Queensland (*Journ. Anthrop. Inst.*, ii, 179; viii, 254; J. D. Lang's *Queensland*. pp. 333, 355–357); Victoria (Smythe's *Aborigines of Victoria*, i, pp. xxix, 120); Maoris (Taylor's *New Zealand*, p. 221). All these examples are not, it should be stated, attributed to fear of

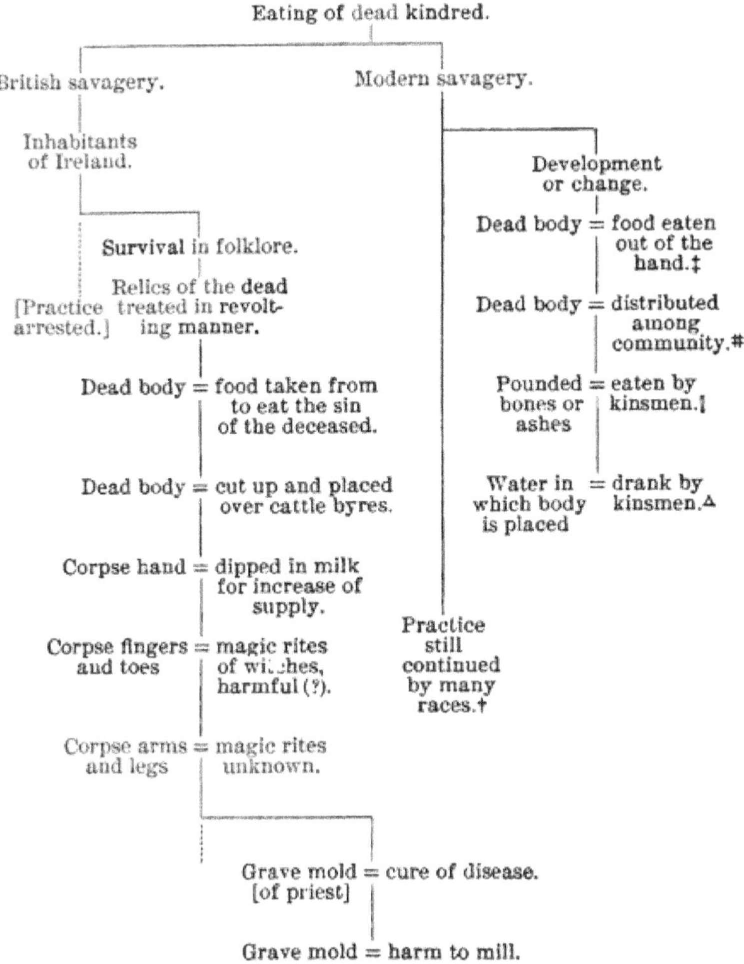


dead kindred; but the whole point as to the origin of the practice is one for argument and more evidence. These examples do not exhaust the list; they are the most typical.

‡ The Kangras of India.—*Punjab N. & Q.*, i, 86.

# The Koniagas (Spencer, *Principles of Sociology*, p. 262. It is remarkable that this custom is the alternative to immersing the dead body and drinking the water); Australians (Smythe's *Aborigines of Victoria*, i, 121; Featherman, *op. cit.*, pp. 157, 161).

‖ Tarianas and Tucanos.—Spencer, *op. cit.*, 262.

△ Koniagas (see note #.)

This genealogy seems to me clear and definite, and its construction is singularly free from any process of forced restoration. Looked at from the point of view of geographical distribution, it has to be pointed out that this group of folklore is found in isolation in the outer parts of the country. The significance of its distribution in certain localities must be taken into account, and it is important to draw attention to the isolation of the several examples. It clearly does not represent a cult of the dead generally present in the minds of the peasantry. A totally different set of beliefs has to be examined for this, and to these beliefs I now turn for evidence of that inconsistency in folklore which I have urged shows distinct ethnic origins. The facts will then stand as follows: On the one hand there is a definite representation of a cult of the dead based on the fear of dead kindred and found in isolated patches of the country; on the other hand there is a definite representation of a cult of the dead based on the love of dead kindred and found generally prevalent over the country.

The survivals of this cult in folklore are numerous. As soon as death has taken place doors and windows are opened to allow the spirit to join the home of departed ancestors;* the domestic animals are removed from the house;† the bees are given some of the funeral

* Brand, ii, 231; Henderson, *Folklore of Northern Counties*, pp. 53, 56; Dyer, *English Folklore*, p. 230.

† Napier, p. 60.

food and are solemnly told of the master's death by the nearest of kin; * the fire at the domestic hearth is put out; † careful watch is made of the corpse until its burial; ‡ soul-mass cakes are prepared and eaten. #

A singular unanimity prevails as to the reasons for these customs, which may be summed up as indicating the one desire to procure a safe and speedy passage of the soul to spirit-land, or, as it is put in modern folklore, "lest the devil should gain power over the dead person." ‖

In the removal of the domestic animals we can trace the old rite of funeral sacrifice. Originally, says Napier, the reason for the exclusion of dogs and cats arose from the belief that if either of these animals should chance to leap over the corpse and be permitted to live the devil would gain power over the dead person. In Northumberland this negative way of putting the case is replaced by a positive record of the sacrifice of the animals that leaped over the coffin. ^ But probably human sacrifice, that pitiable kindness to the dead, is symbolized in the Highland custom at funerals, where friends of the deceased person fought until blood was drawn—

* The examples of this custom are very numerous. I have summarized the principal of them in *Folklore*, iii, 12.

† Pennant, *Tour in Scotland*, i, 44.

‡ Napier, *Folklore of West Scotland*, p. 62.

# Brand, i, 392; ii, 289.

‖ Napier, pp. 60, 62.

^ Henderson, p. 59. Cats are locked up while the corpse remains in the house in Orkney (Gough's *Sepulchral Monuments*, vol. i, p. lxxv); and in Devonshire (Dyer's *English Folklore*, p. 109).

the drawing of blood being held essential.* The real nature of the soul-mass cakes as the last vestiges of the old rite of funeral sacrifice to the manes of the deceased has been proved by Dr. Tylor.† The striking custom of putting out the fire is to be interpreted as a desire not to detain the soul at the altar of the domestic god, where the spirits of deified ancestors were worshiped. And the message to the bees is clearly best explained, I think, as being given to these winged messengers of the gods ‡ so that they may carry the news to spirit-land of the speedy arrival of a new-comer.

All these solemnities betoken very plainly that we are dealing with the survivals in folklore of the Aryan worship of deceased ancestors, one of the most generally accepted conclusions of comparative culture.# I need scarcely point out how far removed it is, as a matter of development in culture, from the more primitive fear of dead kindred. Manes worship, based upon the fear of the dead, is found in many parts of the primitive

---

* *Folklore Journal*, iii, 281. † *Primitive Culture*. ii 38.

‡ The bees supplied the sacred mead and were therefore in direct contact with the gods. *Cf.* Schrader, *Prehistoric Antiquities of the Aryans*, p. 321.

\# Hearn, *Aryan Household*, p. 54; Maine, *Ancient Law*, p. 191; Spencer, *Principals of Sociology*, pp. 314–316; De Coulanges, *Citê Antique*, pp. 33, 71; Kelly, *Indo-European Folklore*, p. 45; *Revue Celtique*, ii, 486; Cox, *Introd. to Myth. and Folklore*, p. 168; Elton, *Origins of Engl. Hist.*, p. 211, are the most accessible authorities, to which I may perhaps add my *Folklore Relics of Early Village Life*, pp. 90–123. Rogers in his *Social Life in Scotland*, iii, 340, 341, has a curious note on the *lares familiares* or wraiths of the Highlanders, connecting them with the ghosts

world;* the worship of a domestic god, based upon his helpfulness, is found also.† But, except among the Aryan peoples, these two cults do not seem to have coalesced into a family religion. In this family religion, centered round the domestic hearth where the ancestral god resided, the fear of dead kindred has given way before the conception of the dead ancestor who had "passed into a deity [and] simply goes on protecting his own family and receiving suit and service from them as of old; the dead chief [who] still watches over his own tribe, still holds his authority by helping friends and harming enemies, still rewards the right and sharply punishes the wrong."‡ And, in the meantime, the horrid practices and theories of savagery which we have previously examined are contrasted, in Aryan culture, with the funeral ceremony whereby the kinsmen of the deceased perform the last rites, and with the theory that these rites are necessary to insure that the ghosts of the dead take their place in the bright home of deified ancestors,# both practice and theory being represented in

---

of departed ancestors. I note Schrader's objection in *Prehistoric Antiquities of the Aryan Peoples*, p. 425, that the unsatisfactory state of the Greek evidence prevents him from accepting the general view, but I think the weight of evidence on the other side tells against this objection.

* Tylor, *Primitive Culture*, ii, 103–109; Spencer, *Principles of Sociology*, pp. 304–313.

† *Cf.* my *Folklore Relics*, pp. 85–90.

‡ Tylor, *Primitive Culture*, ii, 103.

\# This is a common Greek and Hindu conception.—*Odyss.*, xi, 54; *Iliad*, xxiii, 72; Monier Williams, *Indian Wisdom*, pp. 206, 255.

folklore by the absolute veto upon disturbing the graves of the dead.*

These facts of Aryan life, indeed, bring us to that sharp contrast which it presents to savage life in its conception of the family. If ancestors are revered and this reverence finds expression in the nature of the funeral customs, so are children brought into the pale of the family by customs indicative of some sacred ceremony connecting the new house inmates with the gods of the race. I agree with Kelly in his interpretation of the stories of the feeding the infant Zeus with the honey from the sacred ash and from bees. "Among the ancient Germans," says Kelly, "that sacred food was the first that was put to the lips of the new-born babe. So it was among the Hindus, as appears from a passage in one of their sacred books. The father puts his mouth to the right ear of the new-born babe, and murmurs three times, 'Speech! Speech!' Then he gives it a name. Then he mixes clotted milk, honey, and butter, and feeds the babe with it out of pure gold. It is found in a surprising shape among one Celtic people. Lightfoot says that in the Highlands of Scotland, at the birth of an infant, the nurse takes a green stick of ash, one end of which she puts into the fire, and while it is burning receives in a spoon the sap that oozes from the other, which she administers to the child as its first food. Some thousands of years ago the ancestors of this Highland nurse had known the *fraxinus*

* "Choice Notes," *Folklore*, p. 8.

*ornus* in Arya, and now their descendant, imitating their practice in the cold North, but totally ignorant of its true meaning, puts the nauseous sap of her native ash into the mouth of her hapless charge." * I have quoted this long passage because it shows, as Kelly expresses it, "the amazing toughness of popular tradition," and because it brings into contrast the savage practice of the Irish mothers who dedicated their children to the sword. Solinus tells us that the mother put the first food of her new-born son on the sword of her husband, and, lightly introducing it into his mouth, expressed a wish that he might never meet death otherwise than in war and amid arms. Even after the introduction of Christianity the terrible rites of war were kept up at the ceremonials of infancy. Train says that a custom identical with that just quoted from Solinus was kept up, prior to the Union, in Annandale and other places along the Scottish border, † and Camden records that the right arm of children was kept unchristened so that it might deal a more deadly blow. ‡ The same usage obtained in the borderland of England and Scotland, # and it is no doubt the parent of the more general custom in the north of England not to wash the right arm of the new-born infant, so that it could the better obtain riches. ‖

* Kelly, *Indo-European Folklore*, pp. 145, 146.
† *History of Isle of Man*, ii. 84, *note* 1.
‡ *Britannia*, s. v., "Ireland."
# Guthrie, *Old Scottish Customs*, p. 144.
‖ Henderson, *Folklore of Northern Counties*, p. 16.

Not only are these savage rites in direct contrast to the food rites of the early Aryan birth ceremony, but they also stand out against the relics of Aryan house-birth preserved in folklore, and which are centered round the domestic hearth.* The child, put on a cloth spread over a basket containing provisions, was conveyed thrice round the crook of the chimney, or was handed across the fire in those places where the hearth was still in the center of the room.† In Shropshire the first food is a spoonful of butter and sugar.‡

But, again, there is another contrast to be drawn. It is the father who, according to Pennant, prepares the basket of food and places it across the fire, and it is the father, in more primitive Aryan custom, who mixes the sacred food and first feeds the child. In the Irish rites just noticed it is the mother who acts the part of domestic priest. This contrast is a very significant one. The principle of matriarchy is more primitive than that of patriarchy, and it may point to a distinction of race. The position of the mother in Irish birth rites is not an accidental one. It is of permanent moment as an element in folklore. Mothers in many places retain to this day their maiden names,# and this in former days,

---

* Hearn, *Aryan Household*, p. 73.

† Gordon Cumming, *In the Hebrides*, p. 101; Dalyell, *Darker Superstitions of Scotland*, p. 176; Pennant, *Tour in the Highlands*, iii, 46.

‡ Burne, *Shropshire Folklore*, p. 284.

\# Athlone (Mason's *Stat. Acc. of Ireland*, iii, 72); Knockando, Elginshire (*New Stat. Acc. of Scotland*, xiii, 72).

if not at present, suggests that children followed their mother's rather than their father's name and kindred. The importance of these considerations in connection with birth ceremonies is clearly shown by the fact of the survival of the singular custom of the "couvade," where the husband takes to his bed at the birth of a child and goes through the pretense of being ill. "The strange custom of the couvade," says Professor Rhys, "was known in Ireland, at least in Ulster, and when the great invasion of that province took place under the leadership of Ailill and Medb, with their Firbolg and other forces, they found that all the adult males of the kingdom of Conchobar Mac Nessa were laid up, so that none of them could stir hand or foot to defend his country against invasion excepting Cúchulainn and his father alone."* No doubt this legend takes us into the realms of mythology, to the battles and doings of gods rather than of men; but Professor Rhys has shown good cause for believing that the mythological reason for the death or inactivity of the Ultonian heroes had ceased to be intelligible at an early date, "long, probably, before any Aryan wanderer had landed in these islands," and so the persistence of the myth of the Ultonian inactivity naturally came to be interpreted sooner or later in the light of the only custom that seemed to make it intelligible—namely, that of the couvade. Without concerning ourselves about the

* *Celtic Heathendom*, p. 627; *cf* pp. 140, 363, 471, 482, 627, 646; *Rev. Celt.*, vii, 227.

mythology connected with this particular episode, here is the custom itself standing out clearly and distinctly, and its duration of "four days and five nights" may be the period allotted to the primitive formula. It is to be traced also in Scotland. A man who had incurred the resentment of Margaret Hutchesone "that same night took sicknes: and had panes as a woman in chyldbirth."* On the borders of Scotland, as lately as the year 1772, there was pointed out to Mr. Pennant the offspring of a woman whose pains had been transferred to her husband by the midwife. The legends of the saints relate that Merinus, a future bishop, having been refused access to the castle of some Irish potentate whose spouse was then in labor, and treated with contempt, prayed for the transference of her sufferings to him, which ensued immediately.† In Yorkshire, too, a custom exists, or existed, which seems without doubt to be a survival of this peculiar custom. "When an illegitimate child is born it is a point of honor with the girl not to reveal the father, but the mother of the girl goes out to look for him, and the first man she finds keeping his bed is he."‡ These are the last remnants in custom, as well as in tradition, of a singularly symbolical practice, which had to do with some aspect of society when motherhood, not fatherhood, was the ini-

---

* Quoted in Dalyell's *Darker Superstitions*, p. 133.

† Pennant, *Tour* 1772, p. 79.

‡ *Academy*, xxv, p. 112. Unfortunately the exact place in Yorkshire where this custom obtains is not stated.

tial point of birthright, and which, in the opinion of most writers who have investigated the subject, is to be classed as non-Aryan in origin—an opinion which is fortified by its prevalence among the Basque people of to-day, while elsewhere in Europe it is found only by digging among the mass of folklore, and then only in such isolation as to suggest that it does not belong to the main current of traditional peasant life.

Alike, then, in customs relating to the dead and in customs relating to birth there are two streams of thought, not one. The one is savage, the other is Aryan. That both are represented in folklore indicates that they were arrested in their development by some forces hostile to them, and pushed back to exist as survivals if they were to exist at all. At the moment of this arrest the one must have been practiced by savages, and we may postulate that the arresting force was the incoming Aryan culture; the other must have been practiced by Aryans, and we may postulate that the arresting force was Christianity. Thus the presence of savage culture and Aryan culture, represented by savages and Aryans, is proved by the evidence of folklore.*

2. It is possible to compare the cult of the dead, which has just been traced out in its dual line of gen-

---

* Mr. Elton declares for the pre-Celtic origin of the sin-eating, among other customs. They "can hardly be referred to any other origin than the persistence of ancient habits among the descendants of the Silurian tribes."—*Origins of English History*, p. 179.

ealogy, with a practice which relates to the treatment of the living. Human life among savages is not valued except for what it is worth to the tribe. Female children and the aged and infirm are alike sacrificed to the primitive law of economics, and no sacred ties of kinship step across to thwart the stern necessities of savage life.

Within the memory of credible witnesses, says Miss Burne, affectionate relatives have been known to hasten the moment of death, and she quotes a singular case of strangulation in support of her general statement.* Aubrey has preserved an old English "countrie story" of "the holy mawle, which (they fancy) hung behind the church dore, which, when the father was seaventie, the sonne might fetch to knock his father on the head as effete and of no more use."† In a fifteenth-century MS. of prose romances, Sir Percival, in his adventures in quest of the Holy Grail, being at one time ill at ease, congratulates himself that he is not like those men of Wales, where sons pull their fathers out of bed and kill them to save the disgrace of their dying in bed.‡ Here are three distinct references to the custom of killing the aged, and it seems impossible to get away from the disagreeable conclusion that the actual practice has not so long since died out from among us.# Its opposition to

* *Shropshire Folklore*, p. 297.

† *Remaines of Gentilisme and Judaisme*, p. 19.

‡ Nutt, *Legend of the Holy Grail*, p. 44.

# The practice is recorded in Prussia and Sweden. See Keysler, quoted by Elton, *Origins of Eng. Hist.*, p. 91, and Geiger, *Hist. Sweden*, pp. 31, 32.

the Aryan conception of the sacred ties of kindred does not need proof, and I have attempted to trace out the origin of some Scottish and English tales as due to the first Aryan observation of this strange practice of their non-Aryan opponents.*

3. I want to point out that these customs, illustrating the position of enmity and fear between man and man, and opposed, therefore, to the theory of tribal kinship, where men of one kin are knit together by ties which, if not to be properly characterized by the term "love," at all events allay the feelings of enmity, become of singular importance as a test of the culture of a people when the evidence becomes cumulative. If when kindred are dead they are feared as enemies, if when they cease to be of use to the community they are promptly dispatched to the land of spirits, it would be a part of the same attitude of man toward man that sickness would be caused by the devilish practices of men, and might be alleviated by the sacrifice of one human being for another. There is, in the presence of such practices, no sacred tribal life to preserve and cherish such as there was in Aryan society, and it seems certain that this group of custom and belief belongs to a level of culture lower than Aryan. I proceed, then, to examine the evidence for the sacrifice of a human being as a cure for disease.

We start off with a practice performed upon animals, one animal in a herd being sacrificed for the herd.

---

* See *Folklore*, i, 206.

That this custom does not obtain among modern pastoral tribes of savages shows that it is the first stage in our examination, because it suggests that the folk usage is not in its original form, and that probably from the fact of animals being represented therein something is symbolized by them which, if explained, would give us the original form.* Mr. Forbes Leslie,† and other authorities have collected some evidence together, and I rearrange it, with further illustrations, in the following order. Within twenty miles of the metropolis of Scotland a relative of Professor Simpson offered up a live cow as a sacrifice to the spirit of the murrain.‡ Sir Arthur Mitchell records another example in the county of Moray.# Grimm cites a remarkable case occurring in 1767 in the Island of Mull. In consequence of a disease among the black cattle the people agreed to perform an incantation, though they esteemed it a wicked thing. They carried to the top of Carnmoor a wheel and nine spindles of oak-wood. They extinguished every fire in every house within sight of the hill; the wheel was then turned from east to west over the nine spindles long enough to produce fire by friction. If the fire was not produced before noon the incantation

* The great cattle-rearing tribes, Kaffirs, Todas, and others, though they perform various significant ceremonies in connection with their herds, do not, so far as I have been able to discover, sacrifice one of the herd for the benefit of the remainder.

† *Early Races of Scotland*, i, 84 *et seq.*

‡ *Proc. Soc. Antiq. Scot.*, iv, 33.

# *Ibid.*, p. 260; Gordon Cumming, *In the Hebrides*, p. 194.

lost its effect. They then sacrificed a heifer, cutting in pieces, and burning while yet alive, the diseased part. They then lighted their own hearths from the pile, and ended by feasting on the remains. Words of incantation were repeated by an old man from Morven, who continued speaking all the time the fire was being raised.* Keating speaks of the custom as a general one in Ireland, the chief object of the ceremony being to preserve the animals from contagious disorders for the year.† Dalyell notes from the Scottish Trials that a woman endeavored to repress the progress of the distemper among her cattle by taking a live ox, a cat, and a quantity of salt, and burying all together in a deep hole in the ground "as ane sacrifice to the devill." ‡

In Wales, when a violent disease broke out among the horned cattle, the farmers of the district where it raged joined to give up a bullock for a victim, which was carried to the top of a precipice from whence it was thrown down. This was called "casting a captive to the devil." # In Scotland, and also Yorkshire, the sacrificed cow was buried beneath the threshold of the cattle-house.‖ In Northamptonshire the animal was burned for "good luck." ^ In Cornwall a calf was burned in

* Grimm, *Teut. Myth.*, p. 608.

† Forbes Leslie, *Early Races of Scotland*, i, 115.

‡ Dalyell, *Darker Superstitions*, p. 186.

# *Beauties of England and Wales*, 1812, xvii, i, 36.

‖ Atkinson, *Forty Years in a Moorland Parish*, p. 62; Guthrie, *Old Scottish Customs*, p. 97.

^ Grimm, *Teut. Myth*, p. 610.

1800 to arrest the murrain.* Dalyell alludes to "a recent expedient in the neighboring kingdom," probably, therefore, the north of England, where a person having lost many of his herd, burned a living calf to preserve the remainder.†

We pick out from these customs two details, namely, the death by fire and the casting down from the precipice, and note that they are forms of sacrifice specially applicable to human beings. The next link in the genealogy of these customs is supplied by the earlier examples from Scotland. In 1643 John Brughe and Neane Nikclerith conjoined their mutual skill to save the herd from sickness, and they buried one alive "and maid all the rest of the cattell theireftir to go over that place"; ‡ and in 1629 the proprietor of some sheep in the Isle of Birsay was advised "to take ane beast at Alhallow evin and sprinkill thrie dropps of the bluid of it ben by the fyre." #

In this last example the sacrifice is connected unmistakably with the house—the domestic hearth. Accordingly the next stage back seems to me to be the sacrifice of an animal, not for animal sickness, but for human sickness. This stage is actually represented in Scottish usage. The records of Dingwall on August 6,

---

* Hone, *Everyday Book*, i. 431; Henderson, *Folklore*, p. 149; Hunt's *Popular Romances of West of England*, pp. 212–214.

† Dalyell, *Darker Superstitions of Scotland*, p. 184. Professor Rhys tells me this also occurs in the Isle of Man.

‡ *Ibid.* p. 185.

# *Ibid.*, p. 184.

1678, note the proceedings taken against four of the Mackenzies "for sacrificing a bull in ane heathenish manner in the Island of St. Ruffus, commonly called Ellan Moury, in Lochew, for the recovery of the health of Cirstane Mackenzie." * Reference to the same ceremony is contained in the trial of Helene Isbuster in 1635, where it is stated that Adam Lennard recovered from his sickness as the cows and oxen of another recovered.† In an Irish example the interposition of a saint-deity does not hide the primitive practice. An image of wood about two feet high, carved and painted like a woman, was kept by one of the family of O'Herlebys in Ballyvorney, County Cork, and when any one was sick of the small-pox they sent for it, sacrificed a sheep to it, and wrapped the skin about the sick person, and the family ate the sheep.‡

The stage of "animal for animal" is therefore preceded by the stage of "animal for human being." The earliest stage of all, where human being is sacrificed for human being, is, if I mistake not, represented in the hideous practice, attested by Sir Arthur Mitchell, of epileptic patients tasting the blood of a murderer to be cured of their disease.# Here once more the murderer and the outcast are the objects of particularly revolting practices, which appear to have been transferred to

* *Proc. Soc. Antiq. Scot.*, iv, 258.

† Dalyell, *Darker Superstitions*, p. 182.

‡ Richardson, *The Great Folly Superstition, and Idolatry of Pilgrimages.*

# *Past in the Present*, p. 154.

them during the development of more humane notions concerning one's fellow-creatures. But the final stage of the genealogy is more clearly represented than even this. Among the dismal records of witchcraft in Scotland toward the end of the sixteenth century there is unmistakable evidence of the sacrifice of one human being for another in cases of sickness. On July 22, 1590, Hector Monro, seventeenth Baron of Fowlis, was tried "for sorcery, incantation, witchcraft, and slaughter." It appears that in 1588, being sick, he sent for a notorious witch, who informed the Baron that he could not recover unless "the principal man of his bluid should die for him." George Monro, the Baron's half-brother, was selected as the victim. The witch and her accomplices one hour after midnight repaired to a spot near high-water mark where there was a boundary between lands belonging to the king and the bishop. There, having first carefully removed the turf, they dug a grave long enough to contain the sick man, Hector Monro. Having placed him in the grave, they then covered him with the green turf, which they fastened with wands. The foster-mother of the Baron then ran the breadth of nine ridges, and on returning to the grave asked the witch "which was her choice." She answered that "Hector should live and his brother George die for him." This part of the ceremony being three times repeated, and from the commencement to the end of these rites no other words having been spoken, Hector was removed from the grave and conveyed back to his bed. He recovered from his illness and his brother died.*

There can be no doubt about such an example as this. "The alleged act of transferring disease or pain from one person to another," says Mr. Forbes Leslie, "and thus relieving the original sufferer, is one of the most common articles of accusation in the trials of witches. . . . That the transfer of maladies was only a modification of the tenet of sacrifice of one life being efficient for the saving of another appears from the explanation of Catherine Bigland, who was tried in 1615 for having transferred a disease from herself to a man. Having heard the accusation, she exclaimed: "If William Bigland lived, she would die; therefore God forbid he live." †

The genealogy does not end here, for the practices of the Scottish witches exactly carry out the tenets of the Druids, who believed that the life of one man could only be redeemed by that of another. The Scottish witch did not get her creed and rites from the writings of Cæsar and Pliny; she got them by descent from Druid practices which Cæsar and Pliny witnessed or might have witnessed.

In any society where human sacrifice was practiced for the cure of disease it may be surmised that not always could the rite be accomplished, and especially in

---

* Forbes Leslie, *Early Races of Scotland*, i, 79–82; Pitcairn's *Criminal Trials*, i, 191–204.

† Forbes Leslie, *op. cit.*, i, 83.

cases where the patient was not rich and powerful. Probably only in cases of great chiefs was the rite regularly practiced. In other cases disease would be transferred from the patient to a human victim in a less ostentatious manner, and this side of the case is also represented in folklore.

The Orkney islanders wash a sick person and then throw the water down at a gateway, in the charitable belief that the sickness will leave the patient and be transferred to the first person who passes through the gate.* Direct transfer, by the aid of warlocks or witches, was practiced in the Highlands, in which an enchanted yarn was placed over the door where the victim was to pass.† At Inverkip, near Paisley, in 1694, nail-parings and hairs from the eye-lashes and crown of the head of the patient, also a small coin, were sewed up in a piece of cloth and so placed that the package might be picked up by some one, who would forthwith have the malady transferred to him.‡

The transfer of disease to animals seems to be the folklore substitution for the last group of examples. In the Highlands a cat was washed in the water which had served for the ablution of the invalid, and was then set free.#

---

* Rogers, *Social Life in Scotland*, iii, 226; *cf.* Dalyell, *Darker Superstitions*, p. 104.

† Dalyell, *op. cit.*, pp. 106, 107.

‡ Rogers, *Social Life in Scotland*, iii, 317.

\# Dalyell, *Darker Superstitions*, pp. 104, 105, 108.

Finally the transference of disease from one animal to another also appears in this group. In Caithness Dalyell records a case of transporting a portion of the diseased animal from the owner's house to the dwelling of another, whose cattle sickened and died, while those of the former recovered.*

Thus the sacrifice of a human being for the cure of disease has been traced down through all stages of its survival. It is a good example of what I have termed "substitution" in folklore, and is remarkable because it is not only the victim for whom a substitute is found, but the complete rite, originally under the Druidic cult appertaining to man, and, so far as we know or are warranted in conjecturing, only to man, is found in folklore appertaining to animals. Other remedies having been discovered for the cure of disease among men, or an intrusive race of people having introduced other remedies, the older cult is perpetuated by another medium. It is oftener the case than is generally supposed that rites once incidental to human society are transferred under new influences to cattle instead of being entirely abolished, and if this characteristic of folklore be constantly kept in mind while examining animal folklore better results will be arrived at than by interpreting it by all sorts of mythic fancy out of keeping with the standards of primitive culture.

4. Henderson says that the moss-troopers of the

---

* Dalyell, *op. cit.*, pp. 108, 109.

borders made the saining torch for a funeral from the fat of a slaughtered enemy, or at least of a murdered man.*

I take it that this diabolical practice indicates an attitude toward one's enemies which at once suggests that the region of savagery can alone explain it. In the mean time it is to be observed that but for this record the transitional stage from "enemy" to a "murdered man" would hardly have been perceived, and I note this as another instance where the attitude of the peasantry to the murdered and their slayers often represents a much older feeling existing among members of a clan or tribe for strangers that are enemies. Before trying to interpret what this feeling may be, I will see what there is in tradition and custom in extension of the fact recorded by Henderson. The isolated note, clear as it is as the record of a practice that is not civilized, does not tell much of its history, which may, however, be recovered by noting other facts connected with the treatment of enemies. If from the mere atrocities of warfare there may be traced the theory of savage life which underlies certain specific acts, we may, by means of this theory, trace out the connection between the border custom and the practices of savages.

Modern times supply evidence of savage practice toward an enemy which help to explain the place in folklore of the moss-troopers' saining torch. In the

---

* *Folklore of Northern Counties*, p. 54; *cf.* p. 239 of the same volume.

reign of James VI of Scotland the MacDonalds killed the chief of the clan Drummond of Drummondernoch and cut off his head; and the king's proclamation describes how they carried the head to "the Laird of McGregor, who, and his haill surname of McGregors purposely conveined at the kirk of Buchquhidder, qr they caused ye said umqll John's head to be pnted to them, and yr avowing ye sd murder, laid yr hands upon the pow and in Ethnic and barbarous manner swear to defend ye authors of ye sd murder." * That this swearing upon the skull was not the single barbarous act of a particular clan without the sanction of custom is, I think, shown by the superstition, said to be very common in Mayo, Ireland, of swearing upon a skull, in order to get which persons have dug up a corpse recently buried and cut off its head.†

Many barbarities are related in the legendary histories of Irish warriors. There seems to be evidence of an habitual savagery in the following details which goes far to explain the short but explicit account of Border war customs. The Irish warrior when he killed his enemy broke his skull, extracted his brains, mixed up the mass well, and working the compound into a ball he carefully dried it in the sun, and afterward produced it as a trophy of former valor and a presage of future victory. "Take out its brain therefrom," was Conall's speech to the gillie who declared he could not carry Mesgegra's head, "and ply a sword upon it, and bear the

* *N. & Q.*, v, 547. † *N. & Q.*, v, 485.

brain with thee, and mix lime therewith and make a ball thereof." These trophies are described as being the object of pride and contention among the chiefs, and Mesgegra's brain, being captured by Cet from Conall, was hurled at Conchobar and caused his death.*

Then we have the practice recorded of cutting off the point of the tongue of every man they slew, and bringing it in their pouch.† Carrying the heads of the slain at their girdle, first noted both by Strabo and Diodorus Siculus, is clearly implied in the saga, which Mr. Whitley Stokes has translated from a twelfth-century copy, called the "Siege of Howth."‡ An episode incorporated in the story of Kulhwch in the "Mabinogion" discloses, says Professor Rhys, "a vista of ancient savagery," from which I may quote the passage which describes how Gwyn "killed Nwython, took out his heart, and forced Kyledr to eat his father's heart; it was therefore Kyledr became wild and left the abodes

* Otway, *Sketches in Erris and Tyrawly*, p. 17; O'Curry, *MS. Materials for Irish Hist.*, pp. 270, 275, 640; *Manners and Customs of Anc. Irish*, ii, 107, 290; Rhys, *Celtic Heathendom*, p. 136; *Rev. Celt.*, viii, 63. Mr. Whitley Stokes says the heroes of this story "are said to have lived in the first century of the Christian era, and the possible incidents of the saga are such as may well have taken place at that period of heroic barbarism."

† Whitley Stokes, in *Revue Celtique*, i, 261; v, 232. *Cf.* William of Newbury for the story of a Galloway chieftain who took captive a cousin of Henry II, plucked out his eyes "et testiculos et linguam absciderunt."—*G. Nubrigensis*, p. 281.

‡ *Strabo*, iv, 302; Diod. Sic., v, 29; *Rev. Celt.*, viii, 59. Another story cited by Rhys (*Celtic Heathendom*, p. 513) affords the same evidence. It is possible that the curious instances of magic skulls

of men."* Giraldus Cambrensis mentions that in Fitzstephen's time the Irish foot-soldiers collected about two hundred of the enemies' heads and laid them at the feet of Dermitius, Prince of Leinster. "Among them was the head of one he mortally hated above all the rest, and taking it up by the ears and hair he tore the nostrils and lips with his teeth in a most savage and inhuman manner."†

Even among the moss-troopers themselves, whose customs we are trying to elucidate, there are instances both in history and tradition of their having eaten the flesh and drank the blood of their enemies, and a certain Lord Soulis was boiled alive, the perpetrators of the murder afterward drinking the water.‡

There is at least one passage in early MS. histories which attributes to the Irish goddess of battles the dedication of human heads. A gloss in the 'Lebor Buidhe Lecain," says Professor Whitley Stokes, explains *Machæ* thus—"the scald crow; or she is the third Morrigau (great queen); Macha's fruit crop—i. e., the heads of men that have been slaughtered."# Taking

---

preserved in some ancient houses in England may be derived from these savage practices.

* Rhys, *Celtic Heathendom*, p. 561.

† *Conquest of Ireland*, lib. i, cap. iv.

‡ *Denham Tracts* (Folklore Society), i, 155.

\# *Rev. Celt.*, i, 36; Stokes, *Three Irish Glossaries*, p. xxxv. In the story of Echtra Nerai is the following confirmatory allusion: "The dun was burned before him, and he beheld a heap of heads of their people cut off by the warriors from the dun." *Rev. Celt.*, x, 217.

this in connection with the early practices of the Irish as recorded by classical authorities, and the practices so frequently ascribed to Irish heroes in legends and traditions and in early MS. accounts,* the meaning and significance seems clear enough, although I have not been able to discover that Irish scholars have so interpreted it. The story of Bran's head being cut off by the seven survivors of his army and taken with them to their own country, where they preserved it and feasted with it, is still more to the point in illustration of savage custom rather than of mythic thought,† while the story of Lomna's head struck off and stuck upon a pike while his slayers cooked their food goes still further in the same direction, because of the implied custom connected with the plot of the story of placing some food in the mouth of the dead man's head.‡

If, then, the heads of the slain were dedicated to the goddess of battle they would be placed in her temple. With this preliminary evidence before us I want to pass on to an archæological fact of some significance. When Malcolm II of Scotland defeated the Danes, he, in fulfillment of a vow, built the church of St. Mortlach or Moloch at Keith, and built into the walls of

---

† Thus Cuculain's head was taken by Erc MacCairpre in retaliation for his father's head (*Rev. Celt.*, i, p. 51 ; iii, 182). Conall the Victorious cut off Lugaid's head (*Rev. Celt.*, iii, 184). Cormac's death and decapitation are given in Whitley Stokes's *Three Irish Glossaries*, p. xi.

† Rhys, *op. cit.*, p. 96.

‡ Rhys, *op. cit.*, p. 99; Stokes, *Three Irish Glossaries*, p. xlvii.

the sacred edifice the heads of those slain in the battle.* In the Isle of Egg, Martin discovered a burial-place filled with human bones; but no heads were found, and the natives supposed that their heads were cut off "and taken away by the enemy." † So in the interments of the Long Barrow period headless trunks are frequently met with, as are also heads buried separately.‡

Simeon of Durham relates that when Duncan, King of Scots, besieged Durham and was defeated, the besieged killed all his foot-soldiers and cut off their heads, piling them up in the market-place. #

Fortunately some of the practices which mark the savagery of early Britain are distinctive and clear. Beyond the general features which perhaps it might be difficult to exactly classify in the development of culture are certain special features which may be classified with some degree of certainty. People who ate their deceased relatives, collected the heads and drank the blood of their enemies, tattooed themselves with representations of animals, sacrificed human beings, and indulged in orgiastic rites at the altars of fetichistic gods, are within the pale of ethnographic research. At once we seek for the causes of these wild doings. The people who acted in this way did so in obedience to some theory of life which made all their hideous practices good, or at all events necessary, in their eyes and

* *Antiquary*, vi, 77. † Martin, *Western Islands*, p. 278.
‡ *Journ. Anthrop. Inst.*, v, 146, 147. # Cap. 33.

in the eyes of their fellows; and if we would know more about the people who have yielded up their scraps of savage custom to the modern inquirer we must ascertain what their theory of life was. This will not be found in the pages of Strabo and Cæsar and Pliny, or the other authorities who have been adduced in evidence; but it must be sought for in the history of modern savagedom, where practices which startled and horrified the early observers still exist, and in the hands of the scientific analyst yield up truths concerning human life which overshadow feelings of horror. Even the practices performed during the maddening events of war and revenge are the result to some degree of a primitive theory of life which necessitates their performance, and I shall therefore endeavor to trace out from modern savagery what it was that taught early man to revel in the acts which have just been described from the evidence of folklore.

The savage treatment of enemies, represented by the practices of head-hunting and of drinking their blood and besmearing with it their own faces, belong to that widespread primitive idea that, by eating the flesh, or some particular portion of the body which is recognized as the seat of power, or by drinking the blood of another human being, a man absorbs the nature or the life of the deceased into his own.

After the Italians of the island of Luçon have killed an enemy, they drink his blood and devour the lungs and back part of the brain, etc., believing that this horrible mess gives them spirit and courage in war.* The Nukahivahs cut off the heads of their slain enemies and drank the blood and ate a part of the brain on the spot.† Many of the Maoris quaffed the blood of the slain as the essence of life and the source of human activity, and they generally severed the head from the body and preserved it as a trophy.‡ Gallego mentions, in 1566, that a body of five white men and five negroes, having landed on one of the islands of the Solomon group, were set upon by the native Indians and massacred, except one negro. "All the rest they hewed to pieces, cutting off their heads, arms, and legs, tearing out their tongues and supping up their brains with great ferocity.# Among the Lhoosai of India it is customary for a young warrior to eat a piece of the liver of the first man he kills, which it is said strengthens the heart and gives courage.‖ Among the natives of Victoria there is a strong belief in the virtues communicated by rubbing the body with the fat of a dead man, it being thought that his strength and courage will be acquired by those who perform the ceremonies.△

The New Ireland cannibals of the present day are fond of a composition of sago, cocoa-nut, and human

---

* Featherman's *Social History*, 2d div., 501.

† *Ibid.*, *Oceano-Melanesians*, p. 91.

‡ *Ibid.*, 204, 205.

\# Guppy's *Solomon Islands*, p. 225.

‖ Lewin's *Wild Races of S.-E. India*, p. 269.

△ Smythe, *Aborigines of Victoria*, i, xxix; for cutting off the head of their enemies, see *ibid.*, i, 161, 165.

brains.* The blood revenge of the Garos of India is marked by a practice very little in advance of this. Upon a quarrel ensuing, "both parties immediately plant a tree bearing a sour fruit, and make a solemn vow that they will avail themselves of the earliest opportunity that offers to eat its fruit with the juice of their antagonist's head. The party who eventually succeeds in revenging himself upon his antagonist cuts off his head, summons his friends, with whom he boils the head along with the fruit of the tree, and portions out the mixed juice to them, and drinks of it himself. The tree is then cut down and the feud is at an end."†

Among the Ashantees, one of the Tshi-speaking peoples of Africa, several of the hearts of the enemy are cut out by the fetichmen who follow the army, and the blood and small pieces being mixed (with much ceremony and incantation) with various consecrated herbs, all those who have never killed an enemy before eat a portion, for it is believed thatif they did not their vigor and courage would be secretly wasted by the haunting spirit of the deceased. It is said that the King and all the dignitaries partook of the heart of any celebrated enemy, and they wore the smaller joints, bones, and teeth of the slain monarchs. Beecham says the heart was eaten by the chiefs, and the flesh "having been dried, was divided, together with his bones, among the men of consequence in the army, who kept their respective shares about

* Romilly, *Western Pacific*, p. 58.

† *Journ. Anthrop. Inst.*, ii, 390.

their persons as charms to inspire them with courage." *

The preservation of the heads of fallen enemies as house trophies is found among many of the tribes already mentioned for other evidence. The Battahs of Sumatra use the roof space of the village house for preserving the sacred relics of the community, and there are to be found the skulls of enemies slain in battle. † The Montescos and Italones keep the skulls of enemies in their houses as trophies; ‡ so did the Maories. # The Solomon islanders set up a pair of the skulls of their enemies upon a post when they launch their canoe, and the canoe-houses are adorned with rows of them. ‖ Some of the aboriginal tribes of India follow this practice. Thus the Lhoosai, or Kookies, carry away the heads of the slain in leather sacks, and are careful, if possible, to keep their hands unwashed and bloody, and as soon as the conquerors reach their village they assemble before the chief's house and make a pyramid of the heads they have taken; the principal men of the tribe fix their enemies heads on bamboo poles, which they place on

* Bowditch, *Mission to Ashantee*, p. 300; Ellis, *Tshi-speaking Peoples*, p. 266; Beecham's *Ashantee*, p. 76. "The hearts [of the messengers] were reported to have been devoured by the Braffoes while yet palpitating."—*Ibid.*, p. 11.

† Featherman, *Malayo-Melanesians*, pp. 318, 335.

‡ *Ibid.*, p. 502; Morga, *Philippine Islands*, *16th cent.* Hakluyt, p. 272.

# Featherman, *Oceano-Melanesians*, p. 204.

‖ Woodford, *Naturalist among the Head Hunters*, pp. 92, 152; Guppy, *Solomon Islands*, p. 16.

the tombs of their ancestors.* What strikes the stranger most, says an eyewitness, on entering a chief's residence among the Naga hill-tribes is the collection of skulls, both human and of the field, slung round the walls inside; here repose heads of chieftains slain in battle, or perhaps treacherously killed for some wrong, real or imaginary, done to their successful enemy.† The Samoans "were ambitious to signalize themselves by the number of heads they could lay before the chiefs." These heads were piled up in a heap in the malæ or public assembly, the head of the most important chief being put at the top.‡ The Tshi-speaking tribes of Africa collect the jawbones of their slain enemies, and preserve them by being dried and smoked, the heads of any hostile chiefs who may have fallen being preserved entire, and carried separately as trophies of victory.*

From this view of savage practices toward enemies it is clear that something more than mere cruelty is contained in them, and perhaps we may now venture

---

* Lewin's *Wild Races of S.-E. India*, pp. 266, 279; *Asiatic Researches*, vii, 188; Woodthorpe, *Lushai Expedition*, p. 136: "The Lushai have a superstition that if the head of a man slain in battle falls into the hands of his enemy, the man becomes the slave of the victor in the next world."—*Journ. Ind. Arch.*, ii, 233.

† Owen's *Naga Tribes* (Calcutta, 1844), p. 12; Hunter, *Stat. Account of Assam*, ii, 384; *Journ. Anthrop. Inst.*, iii, 477; *Journ. Ind. Arch.*, ii, 233.

‡ Turner's *Samoa*, p. 193; Wilkes, *United States Explor. Exped.*, ii, 139.

* Ellis, *Tshi-speaking Peoples*, pp. 266, 267; Beecham, *Ashantee*, pp. 81, 211.

upon an explanation of the saining torch, made from the fat of a slaughtered enemy, with a description of which this section began. Among savages the fat of an enemy is of value to the living. A very slight extension of this idea shows that it may be of service to the dead. It appears that the saining candle must be kept burning throughout the night, and it seems that the reason for this may well be in order to aid the soul of the dead by means of a light to its last resting-place in ghost land. In the candle which is thus used, made of the fat of a slaughtered enemy who has already had to travel the same course, may be traced that curious idea embodied in the Australian belief that the strength of a slain enemy enters into his slayer when he rubs himself with the fat. In the English border custom the strength of the dead enemy is used to light the departing soul of the slayer to its rest, and the light from an enemy's strength already in ghost land would be a surer guide than any other light. Such is the explanation which the savage evidence seems to me to yield concerning the folklore evidence, and the genealogy of this item of folklore is very short, there being but one link between it and savagery. The question is—Is it Aryan or non-Aryan?

We can only answer this by endeavoring to find out whether the primitive Aryan possessed that hideous belief which taught the warrior to consume or keep as trophies portions of his enemy's dead body because they would make him possessed of his enemy's good qualities, or because they effectually secured him from injury by the spirit of his dead enemy. The science of language is silent on the point, though the refined custom of guest-friendship revealed to us by language * points to some higher conceptions. Comparative custom, too, seems to suggest that the trophy of the savage, afraid of his dead enemy's spirit, had become in the higher development of culture the trophy of the gallent warrior who exhibited it simply as proof of his own valor,† and comparative belief yields the singularly expressive example recorded by Grimm that "a dying man's heart could pass into a living man, who would then show twice as much pluck." ‡

With these preliminary suggestions in hand let us turn to folklore. The traditions of the Indian Aryans preserve a recollection of a hostile class of beings, who go about open-mouthed and sniffing after human flesh, and who carry off their human prey and tear open the living bodies, and with their faces plunged among the entrails suck up the warm blood as it gushes from the heart.# The traditions of the Celtic Aryans are much

---

* Schrader, *op cit.*, p. 351.

† Spencer, *Ceremonial Institutions*, pp. 36–49; the shields embellished with emblematic designs expressive of the exploits of their owners adorned the walls of the Scandinavian houses.—Mallet, *Northern Antiq.*, i, 241.

‡ Grimm, *Teut. Myth.*, iv, 1548.

\# Monier Williams, *Indian Wisdom*, pp. 312–313; Temple's *Wide-awake Stories*, p. 395.

the same. A hostile race of giants, having their sense of smell for human flesh peculiarly sharp, ate their captives and reveled in their blood. The "Fee-fo-fum" of Cornwall is "Fiaw-fiaw-foaghrich" in Argyll, and these sounds, says Mr. Campbell, may possibly be corruptions of the language of real big burly savages now magnified into giants.*

Unfortunately the mythologists have appropriated the parallel tradition of India. They interpret it as a storm-myth of the primitive Aryans. But mythologists have to deal with the analysis of the giant world by Mr. J. F. Campbell, to take count of the facts that the giants were not so big but that their conquerors wore their clothes, not so strong that men could not beat them even by wrestling, and that their magic arts were always in the end beaten by men; and to contest the sound conclusion from these facts, that the "giants are simply the nearest savage race at war with the race who tell the tales." † The nearest savage races in India are those hill-tribes who, like the Lhoosai, teach their young warriors to eat a piece of the liver of the first man he kills in order to strengthen his heart, and to carry away the heads of the slain, being careful to keep their hands unwashed and bloody; the Nagas, who adorn their houses with the heads of their enemies; or the Garos, who plant a tree and avail themselves of the earliest opportunity that offers to eat its fruit with

* *Highland Tales*, i, xcviii.

† Campbell's *Tales of West Highlands*, i, xcix.

the juice of their antagonist's head.* The nearest savage races in Celtic Britain would have been those tribes of Ireland who, as Solinus informs us, drank the blood of their fallen enemies and then smeared their faces therewith, and those tribes of Britain who, on the authority of Strabo and Diodorus Siculus, took their enemies' heads, and slinging them at their saddle-bow, carried them home and nailed them to the porch of their houses †—non-Aryans, in point of fact, as they are in India, who have left a remnant of their practices among the Borderers of England and Scotland.

5. In Yorkshire the country people call the night-flying white moths "souls." ‡ If we ask whether this is merely a pretty poetical fancy, the further question must be put whether such poetry is not founded upon undying traditional beliefs, which have a genealogy of ethnical value. Grimm, at all events, supports such a view from an examination of kindred Teutonic beliefs,# and when put to the test I think the root of the conception in English folklore may be traced back to its home.

Between the butterfly and the moth there is, perhaps, not much to distinguish from the point of view of poetical fancy. In the parish of Ballymoyer in Ireland

* It is not uninteresting to note that the planting of a tree when the hero starts on his fighting expeditions, is an incident in folk tales which bears very curiously on the Garo custom.

† *Strabo*, iv, 302; *Diod. Sic.*, v, 29.

‡ Choice Notes, *Folklore*, p. 61.

# *Teut. Myth.*, ii, 826.

butterflies "are said to be the souls of your grandfather." * But poetical fancy dies away as we find out that the same conception is found in different places attached to birds and to animals. An example occurs in London, in which a sparrow was believed to be the soul of a deceased person.† In County Mayo it is believed that the souls of virgins remarkable for the purity of their lives were after death enshrined in the form of swans.‡ In Devonshire there is the well-known case of the Oxenham family, whose souls at death are supposed to enter into a bird; # while in Cornwall it is believed that King Arthur is still living in the form of a raven.‖ In Nidderdale the country people say that the souls of unbaptized infants are embodied in the nightjar.△

The most conspicuous example of souls taking the form of animals is that of the Cornish fisherfolk, who believe that they can sometimes see their drowning comrades take that shape.◊ In the Hebrides, when a man is slowly lingering away in consumption, the fairies are said to be on the watch to steal his soul that

---

* Mason's, *Stat. Acc. of Ireland*, ii, 83; Hall's *Ireland*, i, 394; *N. & Q.*, 5th ser., vii, 284.

† Kelly, *Curiosities of Indo-European Folklore*, pp. 104, 105.

‡ Swainson, *Folklore of Birds*, p. 152. In Irish mythic belief the souls of the righteous were supposed to appear as doves.—*Rev. Celt.*, ii, 200.

\# Howell's *Familiar Epistles*, July 3, 1632; Chambers, *Book of Days*, ii, 731; *Gent. Mag.*, 1862. i, 481–483.

‖ *Notes and Queries*, 1st ser., viii, 618.

△ Swainson, *op. cit.*, p. 98.

◊ *Folklore Journal*, v, 189.

they may therewith give life to some other body.* In Lancashire some one received into his mouth the last breath of a dying person, fancying that the soul passed out with it into his own body.†

These examples, I believe, represent the last link in the genealogy of the doctrine of metempsychosis, as it has survived in folklore. Poetry may have kept alive the idea of a butterfly or moth embodying the soul, but it did not create the idea, because it is shown to extend to other creatures not so adaptable to poetic fancy. When we come upon the Lincolnshire belief that "the soul of a sleeping comrade had temporarily taken up his abode in a bee,"‡ we are too near the doctrine of savages for there to be any doubt as to where the first links of the genealogy start from. There is scarcely any need to draw attention to its non-Christian character, except that folklore has preserved in the Nidderdale example evidence of the arresting hand which Christianity put upon these beliefs. There is, however, something older than Christianity as an arresting power, and I go back to the Hebridean example to prove that it was at the instance of inimical fairies that the souls were made to transmigrate into other bodies. Miss Gordon Cumming, who records this belief, describes a significant ceremony for preventing the fairies from accomplishing their theft. The old wives, she says,

* Gordon Cumming, *Hebrides*, p. 267.

† Harland and Wilkinson, *Lanc. Folklore*, p. 8.

‡ *N. & Q.*, ii, 506; iii, 206.

"cut the nails of the sufferer that they may tie up the parings in a bit of rag, and wave this precious charm thrice round his head deisul." Here we have an undoubted offering of a part of the body in place of the whole which is so frequently met with in primitive worship,* and if my interpretation of fairy beliefs is correct, it is an offering to non-Aryan spirits. In this connection it is important to bear in mind that the transmigration of the soul into another body is held by the Hebrideans to be the work of hostile powers, and in this as in other branches of the fairy cult I believe we have in folklore the lingering traditions of the influence of non-Aryan people upon their Aryan conquerors.

These conclusions, drawn from the facts as they stand in the genealogy of this group of folklore, are confirmed by the conclusions arrived at by the science of culture with reference to metempsychosis. This is held to belong to that "lower psychology" which draws no definite line between souls of men and of beasts, and which is illustrated only by examples obtained from savage races.† In its crude state it was, according to Dr. Tylor, "seemingly not received by the early Aryans."‡ It is no part of the creed of the European Aryans, and

* *Cf.* Robertson Smith, *Religion of the Semites*, lect. ix; Frazer, *Golden Bough*, i. 198 *et seq.*

† Dr. Tylor, *Primitive Culture*, ii, 6, 7, has collected these together.

‡ Tylor, *loc. cit.*; and see Monier Williams, *Indian Wisdom*, p. 68.

when it is found in the higher levels of culture the theory of re-embodiment of the soul "appears in strong and varied development." All later research by Gruppe and other authorities does not appear to shake this opinion by denying to the Aryans a belief in the future existence of the soul. It confirms the hypothesis that I advance—namely, that in the evidence of metempsychosis derived from its survivals in folklore there is no development beyond savagery; there is no mark of it ever having been adopted and adapted by a people higher than savages; and that therefore its state of arrested development must have been produced by the incoming Aryans.

6. The examples of folklore whose ethnic genealogy I have hitherto attempted to trace all bear upon the relationship of man to man, and it is worth stating that a full consideration of the whole group and its allied items would throw much additional light upon the question of their non-Aryan origin. It is important, however, that I should now give some examples of folklore illustrative of the relationship of man to other objects. In the selection of specimens it is difficult altogether to escape classifying them into the sections which are supplied from a study of the ways and methods of thought of primitive man, but this can not properly be accomplished until the biography of each item of folklore is worked out, just as the biography of words is being worked out. Then, and not till then, can we count up not only what elements of primitive fancy and

thought are represented in modern folklore, but what elements are not represented. And then only can we attempt to account for the lacunæ, and see whether the stream of Aryan civilization has filled them up.

In Ireland, "on the last night of the year a cake is thrown against the outside door of each house by the head of the family for the purpose of keeping out hunger during the ensuing year."* The significant points to note about this custom are the position of the head of the family as the priest for the occasion, and the outside door of the house as the place of the ceremony. The other two elements—namely, the use of a cake and the purpose of the ceremony to keep out hunger—are the substitutions for some older elements which have arisen by decay. The next link in the genealogy is also supplied from Irish folklore. At St. Peter's, Athlone, every family of a village on St. Martin's Day kills an animal of some kind or other; those who are rich kill a cow or sheep, others a goose or turkey, while those who are poor kill a hen or cock; with the blood of the animal they sprinkle the threshold and also the four corners of the house, and "this performance is done to exclude every kind of evil spirit from the dwelling where the sacrifice is made till the return of the same day the following year.†

* Croker's *Researches in South of Ireland*, p. 233.

† Mason's *Statistical Account of Ireland*, iii, 75. "Some animal must be killed on St. Martin's day because blood must be shed," is the general formula of Irish folklore.—*Folklore Record*, iv, 107; Dalyell, *Darker Superstitions*, p. 191.

Undoubtedly we are here taken back by the aid of but two links to that primitive ceremonial for the expulsion of evils which forms a part of Mr. Frazer's examination into early ritual. Almost all the examples —all the really perfect examples—he adduces are of savage origin, and "the frame of mind which prompts such wholesale clearance of evils" is also only capable of illustration from savagery. Mr. Im Thurn supplies from Guiana the needful evidence.* But the closest parallel to the Irish example is to be found among the ancient Peruvians. There is no need to describe the curious ceremonies at any length. For my purpose the most significant part of the ceremony is the preparation of a coarse paste of maize and the use to which it was put. Some of the paste was kneaded with the blood of children between five and ten years of age, the blood being obtained from between the eyebrows. Each family assembled at the house of the eldest brother to celebrate the feast. After rubbing their head, face, breast, shoulders, arms and legs with a little of the blood-kneaded paste, the head of the family anointed the threshold with the same paste, and left it there as a token that the inmates of the house had performed their ablutions.†

It is not possible to connect this kind of ritual with any known Aryan custom, and its dependence upon the

---

* Quoted by Frazer, *Golden Bough*, ii, 157 *et seq.*

† Hakluyt, *Rights and Laws of the Yncas*, p. 24; Frazer, *Golden Bough*, ii, 167, 168.

primitive doctrine of the swarming of the whole world with spiritual beings hurtful to man, and the resulting doctrine of fear as the guide of religious life, absolutely forbids such a connection.

7. It has already been pointed out that sacred stones have a definite place in the non-Aryan religions of the world, but very little has been done to classify the sacred stones of European peoples according to the beliefs still surviving as folklore.* I shall now attempt to trace out the genealogy of this important group of folklore in Britain. We must consider, first, those cases where stones are supposed to be possessed of some magic powers, the exercise of which is not accompanied by any special ceremony; secondly, those cases where the ritual observed to put these powers into operation is of such a character as to indicate the nature of the worship paid to these stone divinities.

On the altar of the church called Kil-chattan, on the Isle of Gigha, is a "font of stone which is very large and hath a small hole in the middle which goes quite through it."† A black stone was formerly precerved in the cathedral of Iona, and it was held in such reverence that on it solemn oaths were sworn and agreements ratified. A similar stone in the Hebrides was

* Miss Gordon Cumming suggests very forcibly that the 360 stone crosses of Iona are probably the descendants of prehistoric monoliths similar to those in use by the non-Aryans of India. —*In the Hebrides*, pp. 65–67.

† Martin, p. 228.

supposed to be oracular and to answer whatever questions might be asked. It lay on the sea-shore, and the people never approached it without certain solemnities. On the altar of St. Fladda's Chapel, in the island of Fladdahnan, lies a round bluish stone which was always moist; should fishermen be detained here by contrary winds they first walk sunwise round the chapel, then poured water on this stone, and a favorable breeze would certainly spring up; the stone likewise cured diseases and the people swore solemn oaths by it. A similar stone was in the Isle of Arran, of a green color, and the size of a goose's egg; it was known as the stone of St. Molingus and was kept in the custody of the Clan Chattan; the popular belief was that it not only cured disease, but that if it were thrown at an advancing foe they would be terror-stricken and retreat, and it was also a solemn thing to swear by. It was in the custody of a woman, and was preserved "wrapped up in fair linen cloth, and about that there is a piece of woolen cloth." *

In the island of North Ronaldsay there is a large stone about nine or ten feet high and four broad, placed upright in a plain, but no tradition is preserved concerning it. On New Year's Day the inhabitants assembled there and danced by the moonlight with no other music than their own singing.† In Benbecula, "the vulgar retain the custom of making a religious tour

---

* Gordon Cumming, *op. cit.*, pp. 70, 167; Martin's *Western Islands*, pp. 166, 226.

† Sinclair's *Stat. Acc. of Scotland*, vii, 489.

round " several big kairnes of stones on the east side of the island on Sundays and holidays.* The same is recorded of the islands of Kismul, Skye, Jura, and Egg.†

Several important facts need to be tabulated at this stage of the genealogy. They are—

(1) The pouring of water on the stone to produce a favorable breeze;

(2) The wrapping up of the stone in cloth;

(3) The custody of the stone by a special clan;

all of which indicate features of a special cult, over and above that which may be gathered from the acts of reverence and processions, which occur more generally. In the case of well worship, it will be remembered that the obtaining of favorable winds was one of the intermediary forms between the more general acts of reverence and worship and the identification of the well as the dwelling-place of the rain-god. In like manner with stones the same links in the genealogy are discoverable.

Thus in Scotland, in the seventeenth century, a tempest was raised by dipping a rag in water and then beating it on a stone thrice in the name of Satan.

I knok this rag wpone this stane
To raise the wind in the divellis name
It sall not lye till I please againe.

Drying the rag, along with another conjuration, ap-

*Martin, *Western Islands*, p. 85.
† Martin, *op. cit.*, pp. 97, 152, 241, 277.

peased the storm.* In the isle of Uist the inhabitants erected the "water-cross," a stone in the form of a cross, opposite to St. Mary's church, for procuring rain, and when enough had fallen they replaced it flat on the ground.†

These examples carry on the identification of stones as representatives of the rain-god, and the rag ceremonial mentioned by Dalyell may without much difficulty be considered as the representative of the wrappage in the Arran example. But by far the most significant of these beliefs is to be found in an island off the coast of Ireland, and I shall describe this in full, as it has been put on record by an eyewitness, though perhaps not a too favorable one.

About seven miles distant from Bingham Castle, in the Atlantic, is the island of Inniskea, containing about 300 inhabitants. They have very little intercourse with the mainland. A stone carefully wrapped up in flannel is brought out at certain periods to be adored by the inhabitants. When a storm arises this god is supplicated to send a wreck upon their coast. The stone is in the south island, in the house of a man named Monigan,

---

* Dalyell, *Darker Superstitions of Scotland*, p. 248.

† Martin's *Western Islands*, p. 59. I am tempted to suggest that the odd custom, recorded by Roberts in *Old English Customs and Charities*, p. 100, of washing a stone figure known as "Molly Grime" in Glentham church with water from Newell well, belongs to this group of customs, especially as it has its parallel in the washing of the wooden figure of St. Fumac with water from the sacred well at Botriphnie near Keith.—*Proc. Soc. Antiq. Scot.*, xvii, 191.

and is called in the Irish Neevougi. In appearance it resembles a thick roll of homespun flannel, which arises from the custom of dedicating a dress of that material to it whenever its aid is sought. This is sewed on by an old woman, its priestess, whose peculiar care it is. Its power is believed to be immense. They pray to it in time of sickness, it is invoked when a storm is desired to dash some hapless ship upon their coast, and again the exercise of its power is solicited in calming the angry waves to admit of fishing or visiting the mainland.

The inhabitants all speak the Irish language, and among them is a trace of that government by chiefs which in former times existed in Ireland. The present chief or king of Inniskea is an intelligent peasant named Cain. His authority is universally acknowledged, and the settlement of all disputes is referred to his decision. Though nominally Roman Catholics, these islanders know nothing of the tenets of that Church, and their worship consists of occasional meetings at their chief's house, with visits to a holy well, called in their native tongue Derivla.*

All these customs take us back to the primitive idea of rain-making by sympathetic magic which is found so distinctly in savage practice. Many examples might be quoted supplying very close parallels to those we have just examined. In the Ta-tu-thi tribe of New South

* Lord Roden's *Progress of the Reformation in Ireland*, 1851, pp. 51–54.

Wales the rain-maker breaks off a piece of quartz crystal and spits it toward the sky; the rest of the crystal being wrapped up in emu feathers soaked in water and hidden.* A closer parallel is found in the Lampong country of Sumatra. A long stone standing on a flat one is supposed by the people to possess extraordinary power or virtue. It is reported to have been once thrown down into the water and to have raised itself again to its original position, agitating the elements at the same time with a prodigious storm. To approach it without respect is believed to be the source of misfortune to the offender.† In Samoa, too, a remarkably close parallel is found to the Inniskea cult. When there was over-much rain, the stone representing the rain-making god was laid by the fire and kept heated till fine weather set in; while in a time of drought the priest and his followers dressed up in fine mats and went in procession to the stream, dipped the stone, and prayed for rain.‡

These examples of the ethnological genealogy of folklore are limited to subjects where two distinctly opposite phases of primitive thought are represented in

---

* Labat, *Relation hist. de l'Ethiopie occidentale*, ii, 180; Frazer, *Golden Bough*, ii, 14. On the altar of the church in the island of I-colm-kill was a stone from which "the common people break pieces off, which they affect to use as medicine for man or beast in most disorders, and especially the flux."—Pococke's *Tour through Scotland*, 1760 (Scottish Hist. Soc.), p. 82.

† Marsden's *Sumatra*, p. 301. ‡ Turner's *Samoa*, p. 45.

folklore, which are identified as savage or as Aryan culture respectively by the test of what scholars have to some extent agreed to define as Aryan. Unfortunately, the area covered by this agreement is not very wide, and opinions are not very settled. Still there does seem to be some sort of level below which it is admitted that Aryan culture can not be shown to penetrate, and this level is reached in the examples we have examined. No doubt Aryan culture was derived from pre-existing phases of savage culture, but when in that stage the Aryan people had not begun to migrate or spread over the earth's surface.

It might be possible to extend inquiry on the present lines into subjects where the test of Aryan research is less certain in its results, and thus bring in the aid of folklore to bear upon some of the unsettled problems of Aryan history. Human sacrifice, for instance, is stated by Schrader to have taken a prominent place among the offerings the Aryans made to heaven;* the continuation of life after death, which in the lower culture is simply a repetition of earthly events in the unknown home, expands into the Aryan doctrine of a moral retribution, according to Dr Tylor,† which, however, Schrader would not accept, if his version of Aryan

---

* *Prehistoric Antiquities of Aryan Peoples*, p. 420.

† *Primitive Culture*, ii, 86, 88. In a sixteenth century sermon, by Dr. Pemble (Oxford ed. 1659), a dying man is recorded to have said, "of his soule that it was a great bone in his body, and what should become of his soule after he was dead, that if he had done well he should be put into a pleasant green meadow."

pessimistic thought is taken into account; Professor Rhys frequently points out where Celtic heathendom seems to diverge from Aryan culture toward the ruder culture of non-Aryan peoples; special customs, like the barbarous rite of election to the kingship recorded by Giraldus as obtaining in Ireland, and others, are considered by Mr. Elton to belong to the non-Aryans; * while Miss Buckland, on good grounds as it seems to me, denies that rod-divination belongs to the Aryans.† I am aware that if we are ultimately obliged to follow Dr. Gruppe, much more of what is now considered to be Aryan custom and belief will have to be thrown overboard, and, so far as my own researches go, I am prepared for such a lightening of the ship. But it will be seen from these indications of recent research, that the scope of inquiry suggested by these pages is likely to increase rather than diminish.

---

* *Origins of English History*, p. 176 *et seq.*

† *Journ. Anthrop. Inst.*

## CHAPTER VI.

### THE CONTINUATION OF RACES.

THE conclusions arrived at in the foregoing pages are, that survivals of non-Aryan faiths and usages are to be found in folklore, and that the conditions under which these survivals are found show that they date from a time prior to the arrival of the Celts in this country—from prehistoric times, in fact. No doubt such conclusions may seem a little hard to digest by those whose studies have not allowed them to dwell upon the "amazing toughness of tradition," and by those who have never wandered out of the paths laid down by the methods of chronological history. But they may also be questioned by students of comparative culture on the ground that traditional faiths and usages found in an Aryan country can not be accepted as derived from a non-Aryan people, unless it can be proved that they have descended through the agency of the same people to whom they originally belonged.

If for the purposes of the present inquiry it does not seem necessary to discuss objections which are founded on diametrically opposite methods of research, it must be admitted that an objection founded on the same method of research can not be overlooked or set aside as nought, especially as two inquiries have recently been put before the public by Mr. F. B. Jevons and Dr. Winternitz, which discuss some of the Aryan survivals in folklore on the principles laid down by comparative philology. These inquiries proceed upon the plan of ascertaining the common factors among the Aryan peoples, and then discussing their presence among non-Aryan peoples on the theory that the latter must have borrowed. It will be seen that the method I have adopted is opposed to this, in that it does not necessarily admit that even a custom or belief common to all Aryan-speaking countries is Aryan. It might conceivably be a common non-Aryan custom borrowed or allowed by the Aryans. Take stone worship, for instance. It is found in all Aryan-speaking countries; in India alone it is found as the special feature of non-Aryan tribes which exist to this day, and with this evidence from ethnography, coupled with the conclusions of comparative culture, we are able to suggest that stone worship is opposed to the general basis of Aryan culture. I should be inclined to argue on the same lines against Schrader's acceptance of human sacrifice as Aryan. It follows, therefore, that the question of the continuation of races after they have become nominally extinct is a matter of some importance to my theory. If the parentage of a given set of customs and beliefs can be reasonably established as non-Aryan, how is the descent to be traced except by means of non-Aryan people, who continued the blood of their race, together with the usages and beliefs of their race? Clearly, if intrusted to the keeping only of Aryan converts, these non-Aryan usages and beliefs would have become so altered as not to be recognizable—the arrest of their development by the overspread of Aryan culture would have meant their extinction.

I will, then, direct attention to the recent researches which go to prove the late, nay present, existence of descendants of prehistoric non-Aryan peoples in Britain. Naturally we turn, first of all, to the most difficult of all subjects, the evidence of philology. No one who has followed Professor Rhys in his researches into the Celtic languages can do otherwise than admit that he has made out a strong case for non-Aryan influences of a distinct and definite nature upon the Celtic tongues of Britain, and it seems now to be certain that the Picts of Scotland and the Scots of Ireland were non-Aryan people. "While the Brython," he says, "might go on speaking of the non-Aryan native of Ireland who paid unwelcome visits to this country as a Scot, that Scot by and by learned a Celtic language and insisted on being treated as a Celt, as a Goidel, in fact, that is, I take it, how Scottus became the word used to translate Goidel." *

This introduces a considerable parent stock of non-Aryan peoples almost at the dawn of history, and that they have never been exterminated as a race may be

* *Rhind Lectures*, p. 53.

proved by the researches of Dr. Beddoe and others, who point out that the features of the dark non-Aryan Silures of ancient Wales are still to be traced in the population of Glamorgan, Brecknock, Monmouth, Radnor, and Hereford, while in some parts of Pembroke, Lancashire, Yorkshire, Cornwall, Devon, Gloucestershire, Wilts, and Somerset, the same racial characteristics present themselves.*

Thus, then, while philology takes us back to prehistoric non-Aryans, physiology takes us to their modern descendants. May we not then carry on the inquiry a little further, and endeavor to ascertain whether the condition of these modern descendants may not help us to grasp the fact that non-Aryan races are in Britain, as in India, a living factor to be reckoned with in discussing the problem of origins?

The senseless and imbecile destruction of ancient monuments has often been commented upon, but the preservation of these monuments has been the subject of but little remark. Who are the preservers—to whom are we students of the nineteenth century chiefly indebted for the preservation of prehistoric graves and tumuli, of stone circles and earthworks—of Stonehenge and the Maeshow? How is it that London stone still stands an object of interest to Londoners, and the coronation stone an object of interest to the nation? The

* See Beddoe's *Races of Britain*, p. 26, and consult Mr. Elton's admirable summary of the whole evidence in his *Origins of English History*, cap. iv.

answer is, that throughout the rough and turbulent times of the past, while abbeys and churches, and castles and halls, have been destroyed and desecrated, these prehistoric monuments have remained sacred in the eyes of the peasantry, have been guarded by unknown but revered beings of the spirit world, have been sanctified by the traditions of ages. Legends where stones have been removed and miraculously restored; beliefs which point to the barrows and tumuli as the residence of fairies and ghosts; facts which show the resentment of people at the disturbance of these unknown memorials of the past, are too well known to need illustration in these pages. But I want to point out that the objects of all this reverence are relics, principally, of the non-Aryan population, and to suggest that the continuance of the monumental remains by means of the traditional beliefs points back unmistakably to the living and continued influence of the people who constructed the monuments. The subject is a tempting one to linger over, and, when properly set forth, shows exactly how the material and immaterial remains of past ages serve as complementary agencies to establish the influence of the old races of people.

There is a less pleasing picture, however, than this to discuss. Non-Aryan races have brought down survivals of savage culture in our folklore, and this has not been accomplished without other marks of their savagery. Mr. Elton has drawn attention to the facts which tell in favor of a story of Giraldus Cambrensis being accepted as true of some parts of Ireland—little patches of savagery, it may be, in the midst of the more fertile fields of civilization. Giraldus states that he heard some sailors relate how they were driven by a storm to the northern islands, and while taking shelter there they saw a small boat rowing toward them. It was narrow and oblong, and made of wattled boughs, covered and sewed with the hides of beasts. In it were two men naked, except that they wore broad belts of the skins of some animal round their loins. They had yellow hair like the Irish, falling below their shoulders and covering the greater part of their bodies. The sailors found that these men came from some part of Connaught and spoke the Irish language. They were astonished at the ships they saw, and explained that in their own country they knew nothing of these things.*

A traveler among people thus described is exactly on a par with the modern traveler among native races of uncivilized lands. The latter might very frequently see in the native villages or hut-dwellings "young maids stark naked grinding of corn with certain stones to make cakes thereof," the absence of clothing, the use of two stones for crushing the corn, both being indicative of the savage state of culture. And yet the above fact is related of the maidens of Cork in 1603 by the traveler Fynes Moryson, who alleges in support of his statement, that "I have seen [them] with these

---

* *Topography of Ireland*, lib. iii, cap. xxvi.

eyes*." An Italian priest traveling in Armagh is reported to have made a Latin distich upon the nakedness of the women.† But an even more startling picture is related by the same author of a Bohemian nobleman who, traveling in Ulster, was regaled by the chief, O'Kane, "He was met at the door with sixteen women all naked except their loose mantles; whereof eight or ten were very fair and two seemed very nymphes; with which strange sight his eyes being dazzled they led him into the house, and there sitting down by the fire, with crossed legs like tailors, and so low as could not but offend chaste eyes, desired him to sit down with them. Soon after O'Kane, the lord of the country, came in all naked, excepting a loose mantle and shoes which he put off as soon as he came in, and entertaining the baron in his best manner in the Latin tongue, desired him to put off his apparel which he thought to be a burden to him."‡

Spenser describes, about the same time as Moryson, the loose mantles which serve "for their house, their bed, and their garment."# They must have borne a most unmistakable resemblance to those of the Toda women of the Nilgiri Hills in India. These people are described as wearing but a simple robe thrown over both shoulders, and clasped in front by the hand, and which

* Moryson, *Hist. of Ireland*, ii, 372; *cf.* B. Rich's *Description of Ireland*, 1610, p. 40.

† Moryson, *op. cit.*, ii, 377. ‡ Moryson, *Travels*, p. 181.

# *View of the State of Ireland*, p. 47.

are often thrown open to the full extent of both arms for the purpose of readjusting on the shoulders.*

When William Lithgow was in Ireland in 1619, he records that he "saw women traveling or toiling at home, carrying their infants about their necks, and, laying their dugs over their shoulders, would give suck to their babes behind their backs, without taking them in their arms. Such kind of breasts . . . [were] more than half a yard long." † Such a sight has been frequently witnessed by modern travelers among savage races. Thus the Beiara women of New Britain carry their children "on their back in a bag of network which is suspended from their forehead by a band; their breasts are so excessively elongated that they can sling them across their shoulders to enable the babe to take hold of the nipple without changing its position." The Tasmanian women carried "their children wrapped in a kangaroo skin which hung behind their back, and to suckle them it was only necessary to throw their breasts, which were excessively elongated, over their shoulders." ‡

It is surely a matter of some significance, taking into account the facts we have already dealt with, that at Broughton, in the hundred of Maelor Saesneg, in Flintshire, the common of Threapwood from time immemorial was a place of refuge for the frail fair, who

---

* King, *Aboriginal Tribes of Nilgiri Hills*, p. 9.

† Lithgow's *Travels*, p. 40.

‡ Featherman's *Races of Mankind*, ii, 51, 105.

made here a transient abode clandestinely to be freed from the consequences of illicit love. "Numbers of houses," says Pennant, "are scattered over the common for their reception. This tract till of late years had the ill-fortune to be extra-parochial. The inhabitants, therefore, considered themselves as beyond the reach of law, resisted all government, and even opposed the excise laws, till they were forced to submit, but not without bloodshed on the occasion. Threapwood is derived from the Anglo-Saxon Threapian, to threap, a word still in use, signifying to persist in a fact or argument be it right or wrong. It is situated between the parishes of Malpas, Hanmer, and Worthenbury, but belonged to none till it was by the late Militia Acts decreed to be in the last for the purposes of the militia only; but by the Mutiny Acts it is annexed to the parish of Malpas. Still doubts arise about the execution of several laws within this precinct." * The accidents of local history, however varied and impressive, are hardly sufficient to account for such a state of things. The persistence of old custom, driven from the towns and everywhere where the Church and State had penetrated, would account for Threapwood and its peculiar immunity, and it would supply us with an example of the forces which were at work during the long battle between savagery and civilization. When Pennant described Threapwood the battle was nearly over. The dregs of the unruly populace he might have seen would probably not present

* Pennant's *Tours in Wales*, i, 290.

us with an extended or pleasing picture of ancient life. But at least we have here an example where law and morality, where the civilization of Britain under the Guelphs, were not represented at all. The only question is, may we extend such evidence?

It is not possible to extend it far on the present occasion, but it is a subject which needs attention at the hands of those who are investigating the records of the past. We of this age are so accustomed to the language and the results of civilization that it becomes increasingly difficult to understand the ruder conditions of only a century since. I shall, therefore, devote a page or two to this subject, selecting such evidence as will serve for example of what would be forthcoming by further research.

In Ireland, at the conquest under Henry II, the natives were driven into the woods and mountains, and, as Boate said in 1652, these were "called the wild Irish, because that in all manner of wildness they may be compared with most barbarous nations of the earth."* But, wild as they were, they gradually recovered much of their territory, and the English remaining there "joined themselves with the Irish and took upon them their wild fashions and their language." Then we have Spenser telling us that "there be many wide countries in Ireland which the lawes of England were never established in . . . by reason, dwelling as they doe whole nations and septs of the Irish together without any

* *Ireland's Natural History*, Sect. 5.

Englishmen amongst them, they may doe what they list." They live for "the most part of the yeare in boolies, pasturing upon the mountaine and waste wilde places, and removing still to fresh land as they have depastured the former;" and he goes on to say that "by this custome of boolying there grow in the mean time many great enormityes; for, first, if there be any outlawes or loose people they are evermore succoured and finde reliefe only in these boolies . . . moreover, the people that live in these boolies growe thereby the more barbarous and live more licentiously than they could in townes."*

This is the picture of uncivilization in Ireland. It is not the story of a poor, degraded population falling into bad habits from a previous state of conformity to the general law. It is the picture of a people who had never yet advanced from the stage of uncivilization. This may, perhaps, be better illustrated by the following account of a definite example of "boolying" existing in modern days.

There are several villages in Achill, particularly those of Keeme and Keele, where the huts of the inhabitants are all circular or oval, and built for the most part of round water-washed stones collected from the beach and arranged without lime or any other cement. During the spring the entire population of the villages in Achill close their winter dwellings, tie their infant

---

* "View of the State of Ireland," *Tracts and Treatises*, vol. i, 421.

children on their backs, carry with them their toys and some corn and potatoes, with a few pots and cooking utensils, drive their cattle before them and migrate into the hills, where they find fresh pasture for their flocks. There they build rude huts or summer-houses of sods and wattles, called booleys, and then cultivate and sow with corn a few fertile spots in the neighboring valleys. They thus remain for about two months of the spring and early summer till the corn is sowed; their stock of provisions being exhausted and the pasture consumed by their cattle they return to the shore to fish. No further care is taken of the crops, to which they return in autumn in a manner similar to the spring migration.*

Certainly the borderland between Scotland and England can not be said to have become civilized until late down in history. Redesdale, says Dr. Robertson, was, until quite recently, a very secluded valley surrounded by moors and morasses, and occupied to a great extent by shaggy woods. Until all-conquering Rome planted her standard in its center, Redesdale must have been singularly inaccessible to the outer world. After the Roman domination came to an end the district seems to have remained undisturbed by Saxon from the east or Northman from the west. In their sylvan fortresses the inhabitants held their own, nay, for many generations did much more, harrying and robbing their more peaceful neighbors. Redesdale being a regality, with a resi-

* Wilde's *Beauties of the Boyne*, p. 89.

dent lord of the manor supreme for centuries, it was found that the kings writ runneth not in Redesdale. Until the time of Bernard Gilpin, the Cheeves—that is, the men of Redesdale—were probably hardly Christians, even by profession. Their clergy and instructors are described by Bishop Fox in 1498 as wholly ignorant of letters, the priest of ten years' standing not knowing how to read the ritual. Among this community of men, ignorant, dissolute, accustomed to crime, debarred by laws made specially against them from mixing freely with their neighbors, having only slight connection with the world beyond their own morass-girt vale, and intermarrying among themselves, it may be expected that old customs and superstitions lingered longer than elsewhere.*

* *Berwickshire Naturalist's Field Club*, ix, 512. "Tradition without being supported by any historical authority, says that the square keep or tower of Crawley was built by a famous 'Rider' called Crawley; hence the place got its name. The tower was, at an after period, the residence of the family of Harrowgate, of one of whom many anecdotes are yet extant, and amongst others is the following: Mr. Harrowgate possessed a remarkably fine white horse, for he was not behind his neighbours in making excursions north of the Cheviot, and the then proprietor of the Crawley estate took so great a fancy to this beautiful charger that, after finding he could not tempt Harrowgate to sell him for money, he offered him the whole of this fine estate in exchange for his horse; but Mr. H., in the true spirit of a Border rider, made him this bold reply: 'I can find lands when I have use for them; but there is no sic a beast (i. e., horse) i' yon side o' the Cheviot, nor yet o' this, and I wad na part wi' him if Crawley were made o' gold.' How little did the value of landed property appear in those days of trouble and inquietude, and how,

I will now quote a curious account of a savage people once existing in Wales, from information collected from the locality for a writer in the *Gentleman's Magazine:*

"I learn from a letter which I have received, that 'there is a certain red-haired, athletic race about Cayo and Pencarreg, in Carmarthenshire, called *Cochion* (the Red ones). The principal personage in the pedigrees of the district is Meirig Goch, or Meirig the Red, from whom many families trace their descent. The Cochion of Pencarreg were in former days noted for their personal strength and pugnacity at the fairs of the country, where sometimes they were not only a terror to others, but to each other when there were none else left with whom they could contend.' From another letter, written by a person residing in a different part of the country, and who wrote quite independently of the former, I learn that 'the race of people referred to lived about seventy or eighty years ago, in the parishes of Cemaes and Mallwyd, the former in this county, and the latter in Merionethshire. They were called "Y Gwyllied Cochion." Gwyllied, according to Richards of Coychurch, in his "Thesaurus," are "spirits, ghosts, hobgoblins," and Gwyll, a hag or fairy. "Red fairies" would, I suppose, be the best translation. They were strong men,

much less were the comforts of succeeding generations consulted! The only property of value then to a Borderer was his trusty arms and a fleet and active horse, and these seem to have been the only things appreciated by this old gentleman."—*Denham Tracts*, 17.

and lived chiefly on plunder. In some old cottages in Cemaes there are scythes put in the chimneys, to prevent the entrance of the depredators, still to be seen.' In a subsequent letter I was informed: 'On further inquiry, I find that the "Gwyllied Cochion" can be traced back to the year 1554, when they were a strong tribe, having their headquarters near Dinas (city), Mallwyd, Merionethshire. They were most numerous in "Coed y Dugoed Mawr" (literally the "wood of the great dark, or black wood"). They built no houses, and practiced but few of the arts of civilized life. They possessed great powers over the arrow and the stone, and never missed their mark. They had a chief of their own appointment, and kept together in the most tenacious manner, having but little intercourse with the surrounding neighborhood, except in the way of plundering, when they were deemed very unwelcome visitors. They would not hesitate to drive away sheep and cattle, in great numbers, to their dens. A Welsh correspondent writes to me thus: "They would not scruple to tax (*trethu*) their neighbors in the face of day, and treat all and everything as they saw fit; till at last John Wynn ap Meredydd and Baron Owen were sent for, who came with a strong force on Christmas night, 1534, and destroyed by hanging upward of a hundred of them. There is a tradition that some of the women were pardoned, and a mother begged very hard to have her son spared, but, on being refused, she opened her breast, and said that it had nursed sons who would yet wash their hands in

Baron Owen's blood! Bent on revenge, they watched the Baron carefully, and on his going to Montgomery Sessions, they waylaid him, and actually fulfilled the old woman's prediction. This place is called to this day Llidiart y Barwn (the Baron's gate), and the tradition is *quite fresh* in the neighborhood." He says that the "Dugoed mawr" has disappeared long since, and the county is much less woody than it was centuries ago. But as you, I presume, are more anxious to have some traces of the characteristics of the *race* than a history of their actions, I have made inquiries on that head, and I find that the Gwyllied were a tall, athletic race, with red hair, something like the Patagonians of America. They spoke the Welsh language. I was fortunate enough to find out some descendants of the Gwyllied on the maternal side, and those in my native parish of Llangurig (on the way from Aberystwith to Rhayader). When these Welsh Kaffirs were sent from Mallwyd they wandered here and there, and some of the females were pitied by the farmers and taken into their houses and taught to work, and one of these was married to a person not far from this place, and the descendants now live at Bwlchygarreg, Llangurig. I knew the old man well. There certainly was something peculiar about him—he was about seventy when I was a boy of fifteen; he had dark, lank hair, a very ruddy skin, with teeth much projecting, and a receding brow. I never heard his honesty questioned, but mentally he was considered very much below the average; the children also are not considered quick in anything. They do not like to be taunted with being of the "Red Blood," I am told. I never knew till lately that they were in any way related to the Gwyllied.'"*

When we come to England we are not any nearer civilization so long as we consider the evidence which has been kept so much in the background. As Sir Arthur Mitchell has observed, if such facts as are forthcoming of Ireland and Scotland have not been found in England, it is probably because they have not been looked for.†

History has preserved the fact that at the battle of Hastings the followers of Harold used battle-mauls made of stone, which they hurled against their enemies. But such evidence has been ignored by historians, who speak of the great battle and the opposing forces in the same terms as they apply to the battle of Waterloo. Stone weapons surviving in use for battle purposes signify that ideas of the Stone Age might survive in use for the every-day purposes of social life. It is not easy to separate the one from the other, and certainly the attribution of a Stone Age culture to some of the peasantry of Britain in Anglo-Saxon times seems to me far less difficult to grasp than the half-poetized descriptions which, when made to do duty for the whole people,

---

* *Gentleman's Magazine*, 1852, part ii, p. 589. The condition of the Welsh population also receives illustration from an article in *Transactions of Cymmrodorion Society*, i, 79.

† *The Past in the Present*, p. 279.

must be wrong, even if they are correct for the governing classes.

It is not wise to depend upon documents with a political bias, but the picture drawn by Dudley Carleton in 1606 is a very telling one. It has relation to the discussion in Parliament about the title to be assumed by James I, and it relates that "Sir W. Morrice prest hotly uppon the motion to haue the King's title of Great Britanny confirmed by Act of Parlement; but he was answeared by one James, who concluded a long declamation with this description of the Brettons, that they were first an ydolatrous nation and worshipers of Diuels. In the beginning of Christianity they were thrust out into the mountaines, where they liued long like theefes and robbers, and are to this day the most base pesantly perfidious people of the world." *

Mrs. Bray had something to say of the Devonshire savage in her letters to Southey. Her picture of the Dartmoor family and hut in her second letter is in strict accord with the account of the inhabitants of a village called the Gubbins, who were termed by Fuller, in his *English Worthies*, to be "a lawless Scythian sort of people." In Mrs. Bray's time the term Gubbins was still known in the vicinity of Heathfield, though it was applied to the people and not to the place. They still had the reputation of having been a wild and almost savage race; and not only this, but another name, that of "cramp eaters," was applied to them by way of reproach. Instead

* *Domestic Papers, James I*, 1606.

of buns, which are usually eaten at country revels in the West of England, the inhabitants of Brent Tor district could produce nothing better than cramps, an inferior species of cake, and thus they were called cramp eaters.*

A not altogether different picture from this is portrayed by one of the agricultural reformers of the early part of the present century. Speaking of the Cambridgeshire fens, we are told that "the laborers are much less industrious and respectable than in many counties. In the fens it is easily accounted for: they never see the inside of a church, or any one on a Sunday but the alehouse society. Upon asking my way (toward the evening) in the fens, I was directed, with this observation from the man who informed me, "Are you not afraid to go past the bankers at work yonder, sir?" I was told these bankers were little better than savages.† As further evidence of how little influence upon the less frequented parts of the country great political events have exercised, we may cite a most telling example in Sussex. There is much to show that the silence of *Domesday* upon the district of the Weald is due to the fact that William's agents did not penetrate into these wilds, and a few years ago two distinguished geologists traveling there were startled by hearing a Sussex laborer speaking of William the Conqueror as "Duke William," and that, too, within sight of Senlac.‡

* Bray's *Tamar and the Tavy*, i, 22, 236.

† Gooch's *Agric. of Cambridgeshire*, p. 289.

‡ *Journ. Anthrop. Inst.*, iii, 52.

It will not, I think, be considered that too much attention has been given to this part of the subject, though it is at the end of our inquiry. The question as to how people act, live, eat, and sleep is closely connected with the question as to how people think and believe. Of course the examples I have given are not exhaustive; but I think they are fully representative and will help us to understand how it is that survivals of savage thought and belief can be traced here and there, and can be fixed upon as evidence of a race who have never risen to the level of Celtic or Teutonic or Christian civilization.

It would appear, then, that cannibal rites were continued in these islands until historic times; that a naked people continued to live under our sovereigns until the epoch which witnessed the greatness of Shakespeare; that head-hunting and other indications of savage culture did not cease with the advent of civilizing influences—that, in fact, the practices which help us to realize that some of the ancient British tribes were pure savages, help us to realize, also, that savagery was not stamped out all at once and in every place, and that, judged by the records of history, there must have remained little patches of savagery beneath the fair surface which the historian presents to us when he tells us of the doings of Alfred, Harold, William, Edward, or Elizabeth. It seems difficult, indeed, to understand that monarchs like these had within their rule groups of people whose status was that of savagery; it seems difficult to believe that Spenser and Raleigh actually came into contact with specimens of the Irish savage; it is impossible to read the glowing pages of Kemble and Green and Freeman without feeling they have told us only of the advanced guard of the nation, not of the nation as it actually was. Yet this is the view which folklore puts before us. Difficult as it may be to realize, it is undeniably true that the records of uncivilization are as real as those of civilization, and that both belong to the same geographical area. The difficulty is not to be met by ignoring the least pleasing of the two records and magnifying the more pleasing. It is to be met by careful examination of the phenomena, and the correct interpretation of the various elements and their relationship one to the other. The examples of rude people which have escaped the fatal silence of history show at least that, if there is evidence of savage usages and beliefs in folklore, there is evidence also of savage people who are capable, so far as their standard of culture shows, of keeping up the usages and beliefs of savage ancestors.

# INDEX.

14

THE END.

## MODERN SCIENCE SERIES.

Edited by Sir JOHN LUBBOCK, Bart., F. R. S.

The works to be comprised in the "Modern Science Series" are primarily not for the student, nor for the young, but for the educated layman who needs to know the present state and result of scientific investigation, and who has neither time nor inclination to become a specialist on the subject which arouses his interest. Each book will be complete in itself, and, while thoroughly scientific in treatment, its subject will, as far as possible, be presented in language divested of needless technicalities. Illustrations will be given wherever needed by the text. The following are the volumes thus far issued. Others are in preparation.

*THE CAUSE OF AN ICE AGE.* By Sir ROBERT BALL, LL. D., F. R. S., Royal Astronomer of Ireland, author of "Starland." 12mo. Cloth, $1.00.

"Sir Robert Ball's book is, as a matter of course, admirably written. Though but a small one, it is a most important contribution to geology."—*London Saturday Review.*

"A fascinating subject, cleverly related and almost colloquially discussed."—*Philadelphia Public Ledger.*

"An exceedingly bright and interesting discussion of some of the marvelous physical revolutions of which our earth has been the scene. Of the various ages traced and located by scientists, none is more interesting or can be more so than the Ice age; and never have its phenomena been more clearly and graphically described, or its causes more definitely located, than in this thrillingly interesting volume."—*Boston Traveller.*

*THE HORSE:* A Study in Natural History. By WILLIAM H. FLOWER, C. B., Director in the British Natural History Museum. With 27 Illustrations. 12mo. Cloth, $1.00.

"The author admits that there are 3,800 separate treatises on the horse already published, but he thinks that he can add something to the amount of useful information now before the public, and that something not heretofore written will be found in this book. The volume gives a large amount of information, both scientific and practical, on the noble animal of which it treats."—*New York Commercial Advertiser.*

"A study in natural history that every one who has anything to do with the most useful of animals should possess. The whole anatomy is very fully described and illustrated."—*Philadelphia Bulletin.*

*THE OAK:* A Study in Botany. By H. MARSHALL WARD, F. R. S. With 53 Illustrations. 12mo. Cloth, $1.00.

"An excellent volume for young persons with a taste for scientific studies, because it will lead them from the contemplation of superficial appearances and those generalities which are so misleading to the immature mind, to a consideration of the methods of systematic investigation."—*Boston Beacon.*

"From the acorn to the timber which has figured so gloriously in English ships and houses, the tree is fully described, and all its living and preserved beauties and virtues, in nature and in construction, are recounted and pictured."—*Brooklyn Eagle.*

*EVOLUTION IN SCIENCE, PHILOSOPHY, AND ART.* A Series of Seventeen Lectures and Discussions before the Brooklyn Ethical Association. With 3 Portraits. 466 pages. 12mo. Cloth, $2.00. Separate Lectures, in pamphlet form, 10 cents each.

These popular essays, by some of the ablest exponents of the doctrine of evolution in this country, will be read with pleasure and profit by all lovers of good literature and suggestive thought. The principle of evolution, being universal, admits of a great diversity of applications and illustrations; some of those appearing in the present volume are distinctively fresh and new.

CONTENTS.



"A valuable series."—*Chicago Evening Journal.*

"The addresses include some of the most important presentations and epitomes published in America. They are all upon important subjects, are prepared with great care, and are delivered for the most part by highly eminent authorities."—*Public Opinion.*

"As a popular exposition of the latest phases of evolution this series is thorough and authoritative."—*Cincinnati Times-Star.*

New York: D. APPLETON & CO., 1, 3, & 5 Bond Street.

*NEW FRAGMENTS.* By JOHN TYNDALL, F. R. S., author of "Fragments of Science," "Heat as a Mode of Motion," etc. 12mo. 500 pages. Cloth, $2.00.

Among the subjects treated in this volume are "The Sabbath," "Life in the Alps," "The Rainbow and its Congeners," "Common Water," and "Atoms, Molecules, and Ether-Waves." In addition to the popular treatment of scientific themes, the author devotes several chapters to biographical sketches of the utmost interest, including studies of Count Rumford and Thomas Young, and chapters on "Louis Pasteur, his Life and Labors," and "Personal Recollections of Thomas Carlyle."

"Tyndall is the happiest combination of the lover of nature and the lover of science, and these fragments are admirable examples of his delightful style, and proofs of his comprehensive intellect."—*Philadelphia Evening Bulletin.*

"The name of this illustrious scientist and *littérateur* is known wherever the English language is the mother tongue, or is even freely spoken. Whatever he does or says comes with a stamp of authority as from one who speaks with power, knowing whereof he affirms. He is able and effective, both as a talker and writer, as scientist or teacher. To those who know anything of Prof. Tyndall's life and labors, scientific or literary, it is superfluous to say that his utterances bring his hearers or readers face to face with the latest knowledge on the subject he discusses."—*New York Commercial Advertiser.*

*MORAL TEACHINGS OF SCIENCE.* By ARABELLA B. BUCKLEY, author of "The Fairy-Land of Science," "Life and her Children," etc. 12mo. Cloth, 75 cents.

"The book is intended for readers who would not take up an elaborate philosophical work—those who, feeling puzzled and adrift in the present chaos of opinion, may welcome even a partial solution, from a scientific point of view, of the difficulties which oppress their minds."—*From the Preface.*

*MAX MÜLLER AND THE SCIENCE OF LANGUAGE.* A Criticism. By WILLIAM DWIGHT WHITNEY, Professor in Yale University. 12mo. 79 pages. Paper cover, 50 cents.

This critique relates to the new edition of Prof. Müller's well-known work on Language. "For many," says Prof. Whitney, in his preface, "the book has been their first introduction to linguistic study; and doubtless to a large proportion of English-speaking readers, especially, it is still the principal and most authoritative text-book of that study, as regards both methods and results. A work holding such a position calls for careful criticism, that it may not be trusted where it is untrustworthy, and so do harm to the science which it was intended to help."

"This caustic review of Max Müller's latest edition of his 'Science of Language' will command attention for more and higher merits than its brilliant criticism. It upholds a theory of language and of its development which, though not taught by Max Müller, is held by the great masters of linguistic science. The reader not versed in the science, nor well read in its controversial literature, will get from this *brochure* a conception of the critical points of the subject which he might miss in the reading of many larger and more systematic treatises."—*The Independent*, New York.

New York: D. APPLETON & CO., 1, 3, & 5 Bond Street.

*THE SOVEREIGNS AND COURTS OF EUROPE.* The Home and Court Life and Characteristics of the Reigning Families. By "POLITIKOS." With many Portraits. 12mo. Cloth, $1.50.

"A remarkably able book. . . . A great deal of the inner history of Europe is to be found in the work, and it is illustrated by admirable portraits."—*The Athenæum.*

"Its chief merit is that it gives a new view of several sovereigns. . . . The anonymous author seems to have sources of information that are not open to the foreign correspondents who generally try to convey the impression that they are on terms of intimacy with royalty."—*San Francisco Chronicle.*

"A most entertaining volume, which is evidently the work of a singularly well-informed writer. The vivid descriptions of the home and court life of the various royalties convey exactly the knowledge of character and the means of a personal estimate which will be valued by intelligent readers."—*Toronto Mail.*

"The anonymous author of these sketches of the reigning sovereigns of Europe appears to have gathered a good deal of curious information about their private lives, manners, and customs, and has certainly in several instances had access to unusual sources. The result is a volume which furnishes views of the kings and queens concerned, far fuller and more intimate than can be found elsewhere."—*New York Tribune.*

". . . A book that would give the truth, the whole truth, and nothing but the truth (so far as such comprehensive accuracy is possible), about these exalted personages, so often heard about but so seldom seen by ordinary mortals, was a desideratum, and this book seems well fitted to satisfy the demand. The author is a well-known writer on questions indicated by his pseudonym."—*Montreal Gazette.*

"A very handy book of reference."—*Boston Transcript.*

*MY CANADIAN JOURNAL,* 1872–'78. By LADY DUFFERIN, author of "Our Vice-Regal Life in India." Extracts from letters home written while Lord Dufferin was Governor-General of Canada. With Portrait, Map, and Illustrations from sketches by Lord Dufferin. 12mo. Cloth, $2.00.

"A graphic and intensely interesting portraiture of out-door life in the Dominion, and will become, we are confident, one of the standard works on the Dominion. . . . It is a charming volume."—*Boston Traveller.*

"In every place and under every condition of circumstances the Marchioness shows herself to be a true lady, without reference to her title. Her book is most entertaining, and the abounding good-humor of every page must stir a sympathetic spirit in its readers."—*Philadelphia Bulletin.*

"A very pleasantly written record of social functions in which the author was the leading figure; and many distinguished persons, Americans as well as Canadians, pass across the gayly decorated stage. The author is a careful observer, and jots down her impressions of people and their ways with a frankness that is at once entertaining and amusing."—*Book-Buyer.*

"The many readers of Lady Dufferin's Journal of "Our Vice-Regal Life in India" will welcome this similar record from the same vivacious pen, although it concerns a period antecedent to the other, and takes one back many years. The book consists of extracts from letters written home by Lady Dufferin to her friends (her mother chiefly), while her husband was Governor-General of Canada; and describes her experiences in the same chatty and charming style with which readers were before made familiar."—*Cincinnati Commercial-Gazette.*

*LIFE IN ANCIENT EGYPT AND ASSYRIA.* By G. MASPÉRO, late Director of Archæology in Egypt, and Member of the Institute of France. Translated by ALICE MORTON. With 188 Illustrations. 12mo. Cloth, $1.50.

"A lucid sketch, at once popular and learned, of daily life in Egypt in the time of Rameses II, and of Assyria in that of Assurbanipal. . . . As an Orientalist, M. Maspéro stands in the front rank, and his learning is so well digested and so admirably subdued to the service of popular exposition, that it nowhere overwhelms and always interests the reader."—*London Times.*

"Only a writer who had distinguished himself as a student of Egyptian and Assyrian antiquities could have produced this work, which has none of the features of a modern book of travels in the East, but is an attempt to deal with ancient life as if one had been a contemporary with the people whose civilization and social usages are very largely restored."—*Boston Herald.*

A most interesting and instructive book. Excellent and most impressive ideas, also, of the architecture of the two countries and of the other rude but powerful art of the Assyrians, are to be got from it."—*Brooklyn Eagle.*

"The ancient artists are copied with the utmost fidelity, and verify the narrative so attractively presented."—*Cincinnati Times-Star.*

*THE THREE PROPHETS: Chinese Gordon; Mohammed-Ahmed; Araby Pasha.* Events before, during, and after the Bombardment of Alexandria. By Colonel CHAILLE-LONG, ex-Chief of Staff to Gordon in Africa, ex-United States Consular Agent in Alexandria, etc., etc. With Portraits. 16mo. Paper, 50 cents.

"Comprises the observations of a man who, by reason of his own military experience in Egypt, ought to know whereof he speaks."—*Washington Post.*

"The book contains a vivid account of the massacres and the bombardment of Alexandria. As throwing light upon the darkened problem of Egypt, this American contribution is both a useful reminder of recent facts and an estimate of present situations."—*Philadelphia Public Ledger.*

"Throws an entirely new light upon the troubles which have so long agitated Egypt, and upon their real significance."—*Chicago Times.*

*THE MEMOIRS OF AN ARABIAN PRINCESS.* By EMILY RUETE, *née* Princess of Oman and Zanzibar. Translated from the German. 12mo, Cloth, 75 cents.

The author of this amusing autobiography is half-sister to the late Sultan of Zanzibar, who some years ago married a German merchant and settled at Hamburg.

"A remarkably interesting little volume. . . . As a picture of Oriental court life, and manners and customs in the Orient, by one who is to the manner born, the book is prolific in entertainment and edification."—*Boston Gazette.*

"The interest of the book centers chiefly in its minute description of the daily life of the household from the time of rising until the time of retiring, giving the most complete details of dress, meals, ceremonies, feasts, weddings, funerals, education, slave service, amusements, in fact everything connected with the daily and yearly routine of life."—*Utica (N. Y.) Herald.*

JOHN BACH MCMASTER.

*HISTORY OF THE PEOPLE OF THE UNITED STATES*, from the Revolution to the Civil War. By JOHN BACH MCMASTER. To be completed in five volumes. Vols. I, II, and III now ready. 8vo, cloth, gilt top, $2.50 each.

In the course of this narrative much is written of wars, conspiracies, and rebellions; of Presidents, of Congresses, of embassies, of treaties, of the ambition of political leaders, and of the rise of great parties in the nation. Yet the history of the people is the chief theme. At every stage of the splendid progress which separates the America of Washington and Adams from the America in which we live, it has been the author's purpose to describe the dress, the occupations, the amusements, the literary canons of the times; to note the changes of manners and morals; to trace the growth of that humane spirit which abolished punishment for debt, and reformed the discipline of prisons and of jails; to recount the manifold improvements which, in a thousand ways, have multiplied the conveniences of life and ministered to the happiness of our race; to describe the rise and progress of that long series of mechanical inventions and discoveries which is now the admiration of the world, and our just pride and boast; to tell how, under the benign influence of liberty and peace, there sprang up, in the course of a single century, a prosperity unparalleled in the annals of human affairs.

"The pledge given by Mr. McMaster, that 'the history of the people shall be the chief theme,' is punctiliously and satisfactorily fulfilled. He carries out his promise in a complete, vivid, and delightful way. We should add that the literary execution of the work is worthy of the indefatigable industry and unceasing vigilance with which the stores of historical material have been accumulated, weighed, and sifted. The cardinal qualities of style, lucidity, animation, and energy, are everywhere present. Seldom indeed has a book in which matter of substantial value has been so happily united to attractiveness of form been offered by an American author to his fellow-citizens."—*New York Sun.*

"To recount the marvelous progress of the American people, to describe their life, their literature, their occupations, their amusements, is Mr. McMaster's object. His theme is an important one, and we congratulate him on his success. It has rarely been our province to notice a book with so many excellences and so few defects."—*New York Herald.*

"Mr. McMaster at once shows his grasp of the various themes and his special capacity as a historian of the people. His aim is high, but he hits the mark."—*New York Journal of Commerce.*

". . . The author's pages abound, too, with illustrations of the best kind of historical work, that of unearthing hidden sources of information and employing them, not after the modern style of historical writing, in a mere report, but with the true artistic method, in a well-digested narrative. . . . If Mr. McMaster finishes his work in the spirit and with the thoroughness and skill with which it has begun, it will take its place among the classics of American literature."—*Christian Union.*

www.ingramcontent.com/pod-product-compliance
Lightning Source LLC
Chambersburg PA
CBHW030322270326
41926CB00010B/1472

*9783744782630*